Virtues & **V**ices:

Embracing Virtues, Resisting Vices,

and

Living in God's Purpose

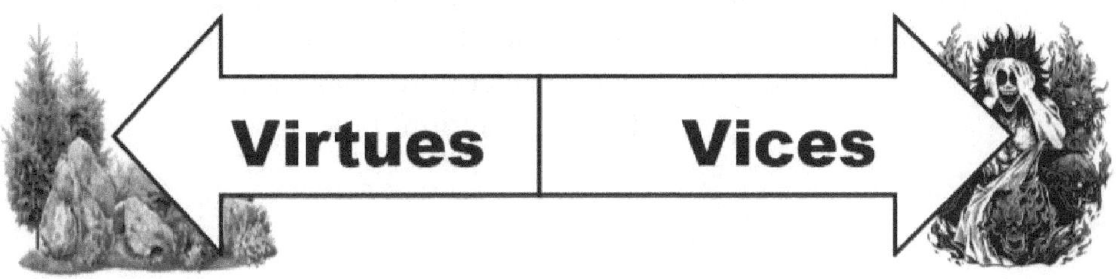

Mia G. Merritt

Why This Book?

I wrote this book, *Virtues and Vices* to illuminate a truth that is often overlooked but is crucial to our lives, and that is the fact that the choices we make shape our lives, our successes, our prosperity, our peace, and even our spiritual health. Every action, thought, or habit leads us down a path, one that either brings blessings through **virtues** or destruction through **vices**. This book highlights these critical crossroads.

Vices, though sometimes subtle, can set us on a dangerous trajectory that can gradually erode our characters, relationships, and connection to God. Vices may give the allure of pleasure and satisfaction but will leave us spiritually depleted and vulnerable to unintended consequences. On the other hand, embracing virtues such as love, integrity, humility, patience, and humility brings a transformative power that enhances not only our lives but also those around us. Virtues align us with God's will and leads to blessings, inner peace, and lasting fulfillment.

I want this book to be more than just words on a page. I want it to challenge, uplift, and inspire you. My prayer is that as you read, you will reflect on your own choices and find the courage to pursue the life that God intended for you. Remember, every decision matters. Let the wisdom contained in *Virtues and Vices* help you navigate life's challenges, avoid the pitfalls of vices, and walk confidently in the blessings that accompany a life of virtues.

Introduction

Life is a series of choices and each choice we make carries the potential to shape our futures and define who we are. At the core of our choices lies a simple yet profound truth: we are constantly navigating between virtues and vices. Virtues reflect God's character and His call to live a life of purpose, love, and integrity. Vices, however, stem from selfishness, fear and pride, which leads us down paths of struggle, regret, and separation from God's plan. This book, *Virtues and Vices: Embracing Virtues, Resisting Vices, and Living in God's Purpose* is your guide to understanding this vital dynamic and how it impacts every area of life.

Each chapter highlights a specific virtue and its corresponding vice and includes a Bible story that reveals the blessings that accompanied a particular virtue and a consequence that emerged from embracing a vice. By reflecting on these biblical examples, you will clearly see how the principles of God's Word are timeless and applicable to everyone's own life. Whether it's the patience of Job, the pride of King Nebuchadnezzar, or Ahab's greed, these stories serve as powerful lessons on the blessings of virtues and the pitfalls of vices.

My prayer is that this book will inspire you to examine your own choices and embrace the virtues that align with God's will. It's not about being perfect but about walking intentionally toward the life God designed for you, which is one full of purpose, peace, and spiritual prosperity. Let this book challenge and encourage you to choose a path marked by blessings that come with embracing virtues.

Table of Contents

1

Spiritual & Natural

Spiritual truths shape the unseen and natural actions bring them to life. True wisdom balances both - faith guiding the spirit, and purpose driving the hands

Although this book was written to highlight the blessings or curses that accompany virtues and vices and how to eradicate or embrace them, this chapter does not reflect that. However, this chapter does lay the foundation for understanding the wisdom that comes with the revelation of knowing how to apply virtues into your life. The purpose of this chapter is to explicate the dichotomy between the natural world and the spirit world. As Christians, we believe that there is one God who has all power and rules the universe. We also believe that God resides in heaven on His Holy Throne in His Holy Habitation. Since God cannot be seen with the natural eye, then by default, we believe that there is a spirit world, and that God resides in that spirit world. According to the Bible, the spirit world is a world that we cannot see with the natural eyes. However, this world is so much more real and alive than the world in which we do see.

The Three Invisible Heavens

The Bible refers to three heavens, but many don't quite understand the concept of "three heavens, so to better understand it, know that the three heavens represent realms or dimensions above the earth in three levels. The first heaven is the first level, which is the physical sky where birds soar, and clouds gather. This is the atmosphere where humans and animals live and breathe. This can also be referred to as the outer court. The second heaven is the next level, also known as the celestial realm, where the sun, moon, and stars reside. This is also the dwelling place of spiritual beings, including both good and evil angels. This realm is where battles, fighting and wars take place, which eventually manifest in the natural realm. The third heaven is the highest level where God resides. It is where every believer should aspire to spend eternity. The third heaven is where we will experience the fullness of God's presence, complete peace, and eternal fellowship with Him. It is in the third heaven where every tear is wiped away, and there is no more pain or suffering. Believers will be reunited with loved ones who have gone before them in faith. Striving to go to the third heaven for eternity should be the ultimate goal of every believer because it will be the culmination of our faith, salvation, and the fulfillment of our deepest desires. In heaven, we will be conformed to the image of Christ, and will finally be free from sin, sickness, and mortality. Our present lives should be marked by a deep yearning for the third heaven and a longing to be with our Savior forever.

The Natural Realm

The phrase, *Everything that happens in the natural happens in the spirit realm first,* refers to the fact that events that happen in the physical world (the natural) are influenced or preceded by events happening in the spiritual world. The spiritual realm is the driving force behind what manifests in our physical reality. Spiritual beings, both good (angels) and evil (demons), do have influence over the physical world. For example, principalities are high ranking demons that have authority over regions or nations. They work through people to control or corrupt leaders, governments, and systems that promote confusion, conflict, and immorality. At the same time, God and His angels work to bring about order, peace and justice. The clash between these spiritual forces happens in the spiritual realm, often leading to what we see unfold in the physical realm. When prayers are made, spiritual battles or actions are initiated in the unseen realm, which later manifest in the physical world. Prayers initiate spiritual battles because they are a direct form of communication with God, inviting His Divine intervention into situations and calling forth His will to be done on earth. When we pray, we tap into the spiritual realm, where God's power, as well as resistance from spiritual forces of darkness, becomes activated. Faith taps into the spiritual realm to bring God's will into physical reality. The spiritual realm operates under certain laws such as the Law of Cause and Effect, which states that every cause that is initiated, has a corresponding effect. This underscores the spiritual reality that things we do, such as prayer, speaking declarations of faith, or even acts of sin can have tangible effects in the natural world. When we pray, we activate the spiritual realm.

Our prayers can call forth Divine intervention that releases God's power or sends angels to act on our behalf. However, there may be resistance from demonic forces, which try to block or delay the blessings, answers, or breakthroughs. This conflict takes place in the spiritual realm and can delay or affect outcomes in the natural world. We may pray for healing or a breakthrough in a specific situation. In the spiritual realm, there could be resistance from demonic forces trying to prevent the healing or the breakthrough from manifesting. This then creates obstacles such as doubt, delay, or physical manifestations of sickness or struggle. However, the more we persevere in prayer and engage in spiritual warfare, the closer we get to the breakthrough. When we send up warfare prayers, we assist in our own breakthrough.

Spiritual Warfare

Throughout the Bible, we see spiritual warfare between good and evil forces. The activities that take place in the second heaven by these spiritual entities influence events such as political shifts, policies, personal struggles, or societal changes. When

> *"Satan and his forces are in constant opposition to God's plans for humanity. Their goal is to influence human behavior, societal norms, and world events to cause harm, division, and destruction."*

evil forces are victorious in particular battles, it can manifest in negative outcomes such as moral decay, war, or widespread illness. On the other hand, when God's forces prevail, healing, peace, and prosperity are the result. For example, political instability in a nation could be the result of ongoing spiritual warfare with evil forces influencing corrupt leaders. However, God's angels work to guide leaders toward justice. The outcome of this battle can manifest in either oppression or positive reform, depending on which forces prevail.

Satan's Opposition:

Satan and his forces are in constant opposition to God's plans for humanity. Their goal is to influence human behavior, societal norms, and world events to cause harm, division, and destruction. This opposition takes place in the second heaven and is carried out through seductions, temptations, spiritual attacks, or even natural disasters. These events are often reflections of the ongoing conflict between good and evil forces in the spiritual realm. These wars are unseen to human eyes but involve spiritual forces that attempt to influence outcomes on earth. The battles in the second heaven can delay or obstruct what God intends to manifest in the physical world, which is why persistent prayer and faith are so important for believers. For example, a person might pray for deliverance from a particular struggle. In the spiritual realm, God's angels may be dispatched to assist as soon as those prayers are initiated, but demonic forces could resist or try to hinder that deliverance. This could result in delays or ongoing struggles in the natural world until the spiritual conflict is resolved.

It is important to understand that spiritual conflicts are rooted in the rebellion of Satan and 1/3 of the angels who followed him in defiance of God's authority. The original rebellion of Satan and his followers was driven by a desire for power and independence from God and a desire to be God. This war in the spiritual realm is an ongoing effort to maintain power over all mankind and subvert God's kingdom. Evil angels, which are demonic forces continue to fight because they still seek to establish their influence and authority over human affairs, despite knowing they are ultimately defeated.

Lessons to Live By:

- The third heaven is the third level and highest level where God resides. It is where every believer should aspire to spend eternity.

- The spiritual realm is the driving force behind what manifests in our physical reality.

- Our prayers can call forth Divine intervention that releases God's power or sends angels to act on our behalf.

- When we pray, we activate the spiritual realm. Our prayers can call forth Divine intervention that releases God's power or sends angels to act on our behalf.

- When God's forces prevail, healing, peace, and prosperity are the result.

2

Love & Hate

Love builds and heals; hate divides and wounds. While love seeks the good in others, hate festers in the shadows. To choose love is to reject darkness, creating light where hate would only leave emptiness.

Love and hate stand as two of the most powerful forces that can be found within the human heart, each with the potential to shape lives and transform the world for better or for worse. Love is a Divine attribute that embodies affection, sacrifice, and compassion; whereas hate represents a destructive opposition, fueled by resentment, anger, and bitterness. Hate stands as a barrier to demonstrating and receiving God's love, because it draws us far away from God and separates us from others. This chapter delves into the transformative power of love and the pernicious consequences of holding on to and festering hatred.

In the Bible, love is not only an emotion or a feeling, but a deep commitment to the well-being of others, often expressed through compassion, forgiveness, and kindness. The Bible defines love as the very nature of God, as it states, "God is love" (1 John 4:8). This truism reveals that love is the very essence of God's being and is reflected in His relationship with humanity. The most profound act of love is the sacrificial love of Christ for all of mankind. In John 3:16, it teaches the ultimate culmination of love as written, *For God so loved the world, that He gave His only begotten Son, that whosoever believes in Him shall not perish but have eternal life."* The Bible also teaches that love is the fulfillment of God's law. In Matthew 22:37-40, Jesus culminated the commandments with love when He said, *Love the*

Lord your God with all your heart, soul, and mind, and love your neighbor as yourself. This highlights that love is an action word. 1 Corinthians 13:4-7 describes how love is patient, kind, and never envious, boastful, or proud. It does not delight in wrongdoing but rejoices in truth, always protecting, trusting, hoping, and persevering. When there is true love, there is light and peace.

Hate

In contrast, hate represents the absence of light and peace and is often accompanied by hostility, bitterness, and malice. The Bible views hatred as destructive, divisive, and in direct opposition to God's nature. Hate is often fueled by anger, pride, and unforgiveness, leading to actions that harm others and damage relationships. This vice is condemned in Scripture because it disrupts the harmony that God intended for humanity. 1 John 3:15 speaks harshly about embracing this vice when it says, *Anyone who hates a brother or sister is a murderer, and you know that no murderer has eternal life residing in him.* This verse emphasizes the severity of hate and its negative consequences. In like manner, the Bible also warns about the destructive power of hatred in Proverbs 10:12: *Hatred stirs up conflict, but love covers over all sins.* While hate divides and incites conflict, love has the power to reconcile and heal. Hatred breeds anger, bitterness, and unforgiveness and is contrary to God's will, ultimately leading to spiritual death. Hate activates the law of sowing and reaping resulting in negative outcomes. Embracing love, as instructed by God, brings peace and prosperity. Always choose love.

Hatred Leads to Destruction

The story of Esther shows the consequences that can happen when we allow hatred to reside within our hearts. In the book of Esther, Haman, a high-ranking official in King Xerxes court, harbored deep hatred for Esther's cousin, Mordecai (or uncle, depending on the translation). Haman's hatred came from Mordecai's refusal to bow to him as everyone else did. Mordecai remained faithful to his Jewish beliefs and refused to bow down at the feet of a mere man. This exasperated Haman to the extent that he plotted not only to kill Mordecai but to annihilate all the Jews in Persia. He was fueled by pride and hatred because of one man. Haman convinced the king to issue a decree for the destruction of the Jews, and he even built a gallow to hang Mordecai from. However, Haman's plan ultimately backfired. Because of Esther's intervention, the king learned of Haman's wicked plot, so in a dramatic change of events, Haman's plan backfired. Haman ended up being hung on the very gallow he had built for Mordecai and in turn, Mordecai was elevated to a position of honor. This story illustrates how hatred can consume a person so much that it leads to destructive behaviors that often result in their own downfall. Haman's hatred blinded him, and in the end, his plot worked against him, proving that hatred never ends well. Check your heart. Is there any hatred in there? Purge it out or it will destroy you in the end.

Love in Action

The story of Jonathan and David is a beautiful example of brotherly love and loyalty. Jonathan was the son of King Saul, and David was a young shepherd boy who was anointed by God to be the future king. Jonathan and David became best friends after David's victory over Goliath. Jonathan loved David like a brother, even though David's rise as a future king threatened his own succession to the throne since his father was the King and he was supposed to be next in line according to tradition. However, when Jonathan learned that his father was jealous of David and had plans to kill him, Jonathan demonstrated his love and loyalty by warning David of the danger. In 1 Samuel 20, Jonathan devised a secret signal to let David know whether it was safe for him to stay or flee. Even though this meant betraying his father's wishes, Jonathan prioritized his love and commitment to David's well-being over his own family loyalty and personal ambitions. Their friendship is a powerful testament to the selfless nature of love, as Jonathan protected David, even at a great personal cost. This love demonstrated the power of sacrifice and showed that true love seeks the good of others, even when it is difficult or risky.

Check Your Heart

Hatred in the heart often reveals itself through persistent negative thoughts, an unwillingness to forgive, or feelings of resentment. It can manifest when you feel hostility toward someone, find joy in their misfortune, or refuse to reconcile. To rid yourself of hatred, the first step is to acknowledge its presence in your heart and seek God's help through prayer, asking for healing and guidance to forgive. Praying for the person you hold hatred towards softens your heart over time. Forgiveness is crucial because it allows you to release the bitterness that keeps hatred alive. By replacing hateful thoughts with empathy and compassion, and trusting God with the outcome of the situation, you can gradually transform your heart and free it from the weight of hatred. By addressing hatred with humility, prayer, and the pursuit of love, you allow God to transform your heart, replacing the destructive power of hatred with the healing power of love and forgiveness.

Lessons to Live By:

- Love is a Divine attribute that represents the highest form of affection, sacrifice, and benevolence.

- Love is an action word that is displayed through patience, kindness, humility, and forgiveness.

- Hatred in the heart often reveals itself through persistent negative thoughts, an unwillingness to forgive, or feelings of resentment.

- Love is an action word that is displayed through patience, kindness, humility, and forgiveness.

3

Forgiveness & Bitterness

Forgiveness frees the soul, while bitterness binds it. Choosing forgiveness lifts the heart above wounds and allows peace to flourish, while bitterness clings to pain, anchoring us to the past and hindering true healing.

Forgiveness stands at the heart of the Christian faith and is a Divine mandate that reflects the character of God Himself. Forgiveness is both a command and a gift because it offers freedom to the one who forgives and can be a path toward healing for the one who is forgiven. Yet forgiveness can be challenging, especially when hurt has run deep, betrayal severe, or lies brutal. In these times, the natural response can be to hold on to your resentment, anger, grudge or betrayal. But when we cling to those vices, we unknowingly bind ourselves to the very pain we want to escape from.

By forgiving others, we free ourselves from the emotional burdens that can weigh us down spiritually and emotionally. Forgiveness is the intentional act of letting go of resentment, anger, pain or the desire for revenge toward someone who has wronged or hurt you. It involves releasing the emotional and mental burden caused by the offense and choosing not to hold it against the person, even if they don't deserve to be forgiven or haven't apologized. Forgiveness is not about forgetting what happened or excusing the wrong but about freeing yourself from the heavy burden that unforgiveness can have over you. In the Bible, forgiveness is a pivotal, central theme, as God calls us to forgive others as He has forgiven us. Ephesians 4:32 says, *"Be kind and compassionate to one another, forgiving each other, just as in Christ God forgave you."* Forgiveness is an act of grace that replicates God's forgiveness towards us. Through forgiveness, healing and peace can be restored and relationships can be reconciled. Forgiving others by releasing resentment and extending mercy brings healing and freedom. It restores relationships, breaks cycles of bitterness, and aligns us with God's grace. When we forgive, we extend the mercy that God extends to us when we offend Him by doing wrong or sinning. Forgiveness is extremely necessary for allowing a flow of God's mercy and blessings into our own lives. We cannot expect God to forgive us and bless us when we are harboring unforgiveness in our hearts towards those who have wronged us. Practicing the Law of forgiveness leads to inner healing and allows us to move past pain, shame, anger, and hurt, thus breaking the chains of resentment by fostering a sense of peace and wholeness.

The Law of Forgiveness is vital for both spiritual growth and relationship harmony. Forgiveness is one of the hardest virtues to apply, but it is extremely critical for building and maintaining healthy relationships. From a human standpoint, it can be incredibly difficult to forgive someone who has lied on you, betrayed you, cheated on you, exploited you, used you, beat you, molested you, raped you, framed you, sabotaged you, undermined you, etc. But with God's help, you can do it and in doing so, you strengthen your own character and knock down spiritual barriers that are put up in the spirit realm preventing you from going so far. It takes everything inside of a person to forgive those things just mentioned and even worse things than those; but having the inner strength to do so shows a wisdom and understanding that everyone is flawed and makes mistakes. Forgiveness makes room to grow in maturity and wisdom and creates a pathway for reconciliation.

The Detriment of Unforgiveness

By contrast, unforgiveness is the greatest obstacle to complete healing. Without forgiving, total healing is impossible. Forgiveness is the foundation upon which healing emerges. The inability to forgive has been the most widespread sin that blocks total deliverance from occurring. Unforgiveness is a heavy burden. When you finally get rid of it, you feel so much lighter. You are a happier and healthier person. Forgiveness brings restoration, healing, and peace. Unforgiveness is one of the primary tools that Satan uses to gain a foothold into a believer's life. He is very strategic. He works somewhat like this: You love the Lord. Your life is predicated upon praise, worship, fasting and loving your sisters and brothers in Christ. Satan has to stop your effectiveness in the spirit because you are advancing the kingdom of God too much. He enters into a person and uses them to hurt you deeply. The seed of hurt, disappointment and anger has now been planted in you. The offense against you was too much to forgive, so you hold on to the bitterness and unforgiveness towards that person. Unforgiveness is now a part of you and is something that you are holding on to. Your prayers are now hindered. You are no longer as powerful in the spirit as you once were, but you are trying to move forward in the manner you were prior to the hurt, but you can't because unforgiveness has taken root in you and until you deal with the issue and sincerely forgive, you will never be as effective in the spirit as you once were.

Unforgiveness is also one of the most pernicious causes that gives an opening for disease to manifest. People have tumors, ulcers, dis-ease and do not understand where they came from. That is because from a spiritual perspective, the seed of unforgiveness that was planted in them eventually sprouted, grew up and became a tumor or ulcer. We don't get ulcers by what we eat, we get ulcers by what's eating us. Unforgiveness keeps a person in bondage and is a stronghold, having a very "strong" "hold" on a person. Forgiveness does not have to mean reconciliation; it simply means release. Forgiveness is a one-sided decision because the main person who needs to forgive is the one who was deeply offended or hurt the most. You do not need permission from the other person in order to forgive them. You simply *release* what they did from your consciousness. When you think about their offense towards you and you no longer feel a deep anger, sadness, shame or disappointment, then you know you have released it. Forgiveness is simply a decision made to let it go. No, it is not easy, but it is not as hard as the devil makes it seem either. It can be done.

Bitterness

Bitterness is an outgrowth of unforgiveness. The unwillingness to let go of the offense allows negative emotions to fester in your heart, which leads to bitterness. Bitterness is a deep, prolonged feeling of resentment and hostility that takes root in you when unforgiveness is left unresolved. Unforgiveness might initially be about a specific situation or person, but bitterness grows and becomes more pervasive, affecting your entire outlook on life and relationships. Bitterness can create emotional and spiritual blockages, making it difficult to experience peace, joy, or healthy relationships. The Bible warns us against bitterness because it can be destructive both to the person holding onto it and also to those around you. Hebrews 12:15 talks about bitterness when it says, *"See to it that no one falls short of the grace of God and that no bitter root grows up to cause trouble and defile many."* This verse illustrates how bitterness is a "bitter root" and if left unchecked, can spread and cause harm, not only to the person who has it, but also to others.

A Dangerous Vice

Bitterness is a dangerous vice that can lead to physical and emotional turmoil. It may cause chronic stress, anxiety, and anger, which can contribute to a host of physical ailments and health problems such as headaches and ulcers. Over time, bitterness can also increase the risk of other stress-related illnesses. Unbeknownst to the person who harbors bitterness in their heart, they become trapped in a cycle of anger and resentment. This constant dwelling on past hurts leads to unhappiness, mental exhaustion, and even depression. People consumed by bitterness often struggle to maintain

> *"Unforgiveness is one of the primary tools that Satan uses to gain a stronghold into a believer's life. He is very strategic."*

healthy relationships because the constant negativity makes it difficult to trust or connect with others, leading to isolation, misunderstandings, and strained relationships. Bitterness keeps a person focused on past offenses rather than moving forward in faith. This stagnation prevents spiritual growth and blocks the person from fully experiencing God's love and purpose for their life.

Practicing forgiveness and releasing bitterness is critical for both emotional well-being and spiritual growth. When we forgive, we free ourselves from the heavy burdens of resentment and negative emotions that can weigh us down and affect our most cherished relationships. By forgiving, we align ourselves with God's will, and allow His love, peace, and healing to flow into our lives. Forgiveness opens the door to inner peace, renewed relationships, and spiritual freedom, ultimately leading to a more fulfilling and joyful life.

The Harmful Effects of Bitterness

David was married to the daughter of King Saul whose name was Michal. In the book of 2 Samuel 6:14-23, there is a story about how she allowed herself to grow a "bitter root" of bitterness in her heart towards her husband David because he exposed himself when his outer garments fell off as he was dancing. He was very happy because he had brought the Ark of the Covenant back to Jerusalem. The Ark of the Covenant had been kept in the house of Abinadab for about 20 years. It had been taken there after the Philistines captured it in battle, but they ended up returning it because of the plagues it brought upon them. After David brought it to Jerusalem, he danced before the Lord with all his might in a spirit of gratitude and joy. He danced so much and so hard that he inadvertently exposed himself when his outer garments fell off. His wife Michal saw this and despised him in her heart (bitterness).

When David returned home, she confronted him and criticized him for behaving in what she thought was an undignified manner for a king. She said, *How glorious was the king of Israel, who uncovered himself today in the eyes of the handmaids of his servants, as one of the vain fellows shamelessly uncovereth himself!* (2 Samuel 6:20).

Michal's contempt and bitterness toward David in this moment are clear. After this, her attitude was never resolved, and the Bible reveals that because of her bitter heart, she remained childless for the rest of her life (2 Samuel 6:23). This barrenness could be seen as a lasting consequence of her hardened heart and inability or refusal to reconcile with or forgive her husband for what she perceived as "undignified." This story demonstrates how bitterness and disdain can create estrangement in relationships, resembling the essence of unforgiveness.

The Great Power of Forgiveness

A beautiful story of forgiveness between Jacob and Esau is illustrated in the book of Genesis. Jacob and Esau were the twin sons of Isaac. They became estranged after Jacob and his mother deceived their father and stole Esau's birthright and ultimate blessing. This betrayal caused deeply rooted anger and bitterness in Esau, who vowed to kill his brother, Jacob. This threat forced Jacob to flee from his home. The brothers remained separated for over 20 years, with Esau living in Edom and Jacob building his life in Haran. Several years later, when Jacob returned to his homeland, he feared Esau's wrath and revenge. However, when they met, instead of anger and hostility, Esau ran to embrace his brother, forgiving him for his offense of stealing his birthright. Their reunion had tears, regret, but also reconciliation. Esau's forgiveness towards his brother broke the cycle of hatred and prevented a catastrophe that could have led to death, destruction, and lots of bloodshed. Esau's willingness to forgive Jacob restored their relationship and brought peace between them, showing the power of forgiveness to heal even deep wounds.

As you close this chapter on the virtue of forgiveness and the vice of bitterness, take a moment to search your heart. Reflect on anyone you need to forgive and acknowledge any "bitter roots" that may be inside you. Consider the insights shared within this chapter about how bitterness can harm both your emotional and spiritual well-being and weigh you down with unnecessary burdens. By choosing to forgive and release those resentments, you will free yourself from heavy burdens and knock down the walls that may have been blocking your blessings. By doing so, you will create space for peace, healing, and the abundance of God's favor to flow into your life.

Lessons to Live By:

- By forgiving others, we free ourselves from the emotional burdens that can weigh us down spiritually and emotionally.

- Unforgiveness is one of the most significant causes of disease. We don't get ulcers by what we eat. We get ulcers by what's eating us.

- Bitterness is a deep, prolonged feeling of resentment and hostility that takes root in you when unforgiveness is left unresolved.

- Practicing forgiveness and releasing bitterness is critical for both emotional well-being and spiritual growth.

- By choosing to forgive and release those resentments, you will free yourself from heavy burdens and knock down the walls that may have been blocking your blessings.

4

Faith & Fear

Faith empowers us to move forward with trust, while fear holds us captive to doubt. When faith rises, fear diminishes, guiding us to act boldly, anchored in the assurance that God walks with us.

Faith and fear often stand at opposite extremes of our experiences, especially when we face the trials and challenges that life throws our way. Think of faith as a light that shines through the darkness that guides us when we feel lost or uncertain. It encourages us to trust that something good is on the horizon, even when the present feels overwhelming. On the other hand, fear tends to pull us back, filling our minds with "what if" scenarios that keep us stuck in hesitation and doubt. Faith and fear are often considered opposites because they represent fundamentally different approaches to trials, tribulations, difficulties, uncertainties, and the unknown. Faith represents trust and belief in positive outcomes, regardless of how things seem to be going in the natural. It fosters hope and encourages proactive behavior. In contrast, fear is rooted in doubt and anxiety and leads to procrastination and a focus on negative possibilities.

While faith creates growth and resilience, fear can paralyze and hinder progress and positive change. In my book, 'Divine Principles; Building Life on the Solid Foundation of Spiritual Truths', I discuss the Law of Faith by stating, *Activating the Law of Faith in your life requires more than just belief; it is a demonstrative act of trust in the unseen God. Faith is the foundation upon which all positive outcomes are built, and it must be nurtured daily.* Faith is the main cornerstone of Christianity upon which every belief that makes us Christians is built. Without faith, there is no way that anyone can call themselves Christian because our faith is birthed out of our beliefs.

The Contrast

Faith and belief are closely related, but they do differ in depth and application. Beliefs are things that people hold to be true without necessarily having any solid or tangible evidence to prove it. They are often based on personal experiences and things that we have been taught, learned and inoculated with. Faith includes belief, but it goes beyond only believing. Faith encompasses a convictional knowing in something or someone without seeing any evidence of it in the natural. If I were to define faith in my own words, I would say that faith is "convictional and unwavering belief." By contrast, fear is a powerful feeling that can hinder personal growth and progress. The Bible addresses fear numerous times, emphasizing that it can lead to paralysis and inaction. Fear often paralyzes people by creating anxiety about the future and causing them to focus on negative outcomes and not act at all when they need to be making important decisions. This can result in avoidance behavior, where one hesitates to take risks or pursue opportunities due to the overwhelming dread of failure or fear of the unknown. In contrast, faith represents trust and confidence in God and in the belief of positive possibilities. Faith and fear cannot coexist because where fear enters, faith diminishes, and vice versa. This dichotomy illustrates the spiritual principle that embracing faith allows us to overcome fear, empowering us to move forward and fulfill our potential in life. 2 Timothy 1:7 states, *For God hath not given us the spirit of fear; but of power, and of love, and of a sound mind.* This scripture clearly reveals that fear is a spirit, and not a good one!

Be it Unto me According to thy Word!

I love the beautiful story in the Bible of Mary, the mother of Jesus in the book of Luke (1:26-38). The story unfolds when the messenger angel Gabriel visited Mary, a young virgin who was engaged to Joseph. The angel announced to her that she would conceive a child by the Holy Spirit. Gabriel reassured Mary that this miraculous event was part of God's Divine plan. He explained that her child would be called the Son of God and would be a Savior to the world. Mary responded to the angel's message with no hesitation, remarkable faith and immediate acceptance. Despite the seeming impossibility of this happening in the natural and the societal implications of her situation, she still proclaimed, *Behold the handmaid of the Lord; be it unto me according to thy word!* (Luke 1:38). If translated in modern day English vernacular, she would have said. *I am the servant of the Lord! Let it happen just like you said it!* This declaration solidified Mary's unwavering belief and faith in the angel's message and demonstrated her complete trust in God's purpose. Her faith not only embraced the angel's message without any doubt but also set the stage for the fulfillment of God's promise. She became the mother of Jesus and fulfilled the prophecy of bringing forth our Savior into the world. Her response demonstrated the power of faith in accepting God's Divine will and illustrating that embracing faith can lead to the miraculous.

The Wicked Servant

The Parable of the Talents, found in Matthew 25:14-30, highlights the importance of using your gifts wisely. In the story, before going on a journey, a master entrusted his servants with different amounts of talents, which at the time were a form of money. Two servants invested theirs and doubled the amounts they were given, while the third servant who was paralyzed by fear, buried his talent and hid it rather than trying to do something to enhance it. When the master returned, he praised the first two servants for their diligence and rewarded them. However, he called the third servant "wicked" excoriating him for failing to invest the talent he was given. The devastating result of this servant's fear illustrated how fear can lead to missed opportunities and dire consequences. This parable underscores the necessity of working to eradicate fear and cultivating faith. Fear can paralyze you and prevent you from fulfilling your potential. Once you gradually overcome fear, take risks, and embrace your gifts and abilities, you will discover that faithfulness in little things can lead to greater responsibilities and blessings.

The potential outcomes of faith are positive and transformative. When you exercise faith, you experience increased resilience, hope, and a sense of purpose. Conversely, the potential outcomes of fear tend to be negative and limiting. Fear can cause you to avoid risks and opportunities, which may hinder personal growth and success. It often leads to anxiety, doubt, and a lack of confidence, resulting in missed chances and stagnation. Fear can also create a cycle of negativity that impacts decision-making and relationships, preventing you from realizing your dreams and aspirations. While faith opens doors to growth and fulfillment, fear can close them. Embracing faith over fear is essential for a fulfilling and impactful life.

Lessons to Live By:

- Faith represents trust and belief in positive outcomes, regardless of how things seem to be going in the natural.

- Fear often paralyzes people by creating anxiety about the future, causing them to focus on negative outcomes.

- The potential outcomes of faith are positive and transformative. When you exercise faith, you experience increased resilience, hope, and a sense of purpose.

- Fear can paralyze you, causing you to avoid risks and opportunities, which may hinder personal growth and success.

- Faith encompasses a convictional knowing in something or someone without seeing any evidence of it in the natural.

5

Wisdom & Foolishness

Wisdom discerns truth and leads to peace, while foolishness ignores understanding and invites trouble. Choosing wisdom builds a steady path forward, while foolishness blinds the heart, leaving it vulnerable to missteps and regret.

Wisdom and foolishness represent two paths that we can choose in our journey through life. However, you must understand that each path leads to very different destinations. Wisdom leads to a destination of peace, joy and blessings; Foolishness leads to trouble, problems and struggle. Wisdom is more than just knowing what to do; it's the art of making choices that reflect self-awareness and an awareness of the world around us. Wisdom is the quiet voice that guides us to pause and reflect before acting. It enables us to learn from past experiences as well as from the experiences of others. Wisdom embodies qualities such as self-awareness, compassion, humility, patience, and a willingness to learn. It is often displayed through sound judgement, compassion, patience, and the capacity to learn from both successes and failures. Unlike common sense, which relies on practical and straightforward thinking based on everyday experiences, wisdom requires a deeper level of revelation and insight. While common sense can guide basic decision-making, true wisdom involves a more reflective and comprehensive approach to understanding life's complexities.

In the Bible, wisdom is predicated on reverence for God, as seen in Proverbs 9:10, which states, *The fear of the Lord is the beginning of wisdom.* This fear is not about being afraid, but about having profound respect and love for God, which leads to a life guided by Him. King Solomon is renowned for his wisdom, having asked God for discernment and understanding to govern the people effectively (1 Kings 3:5-14).

Worldly and Godly Wisdom

God's Wisdom, also called Divine wisdom is the highest form of wisdom because it is rooted in the nature and character of God and provides eternal truth and moral guidance. Godly wisdom involves discernment that goes beyond intellectual knowledge but focuses on living in accordance with Divine principles. Divine Wisdom is the highest form of wisdom because it originates from God Himself. Proverbs 2:6 states, *For the Lord gives wisdom; out of His mouth come knowledge and understanding.* God's wisdom is perfect, eternal, unchanging and provides guidance that leads to righteousness, peace, and fulfillment. God's wisdom gives you insight that others don't have. It reveals information that only God knows. It leads you to go home a different direction from the route you take on a daily basis. God's wisdom is the ultimate wisdom because it is a revelation of things not known, but guides, protects and produces understanding and deep insight.

This type of wisdom is based on human reasoning and experiences. It emphasizes intelligence, education, and skillsets, both innate and practical. However, worldly wisdom may lack moral or spiritual depth. James 3:15 describes worldly wisdom as, "earthly, unspiritual and demonic," indicating that it can lead to selfish ambitions and conflicts with God's principles rather than aligning with them. Worldly wisdom may lead to good decisions in certain circumstances, but it can also fall short of the deeper truths and moral clarity found in Godly wisdom. Human wisdom is inadequate when faced with spiritual or moral dilemmas.

Foolishness and Ignorance

The opposite of wisdom is foolishness, ignorance, or stupidity. While wisdom embodies sound judgment, discernment, and the application of knowledge in a way that aligns with moral and ethical principles, foolishness often rushes headlong into decisions without considering the consequences, relying on impulse rather than insight. Foolishness can manifest as a lack of understanding or an unwillingness to learn from past mistakes. The lack of wisdom is evident in one who refuses to seek knowledge or understand the deeper reasons for the cause of situations. The person who lacks wisdom has overconfidence in their own reasoning without recognizing their limitations. They focus solely on immediate gratification or superficial outcomes, rather than considering long-term implications. The book of Proverbs frequently contrasts wisdom and foolishness, illustrating the destructive consequences of foolish choices, such as in Proverbs 1:7, where it states, *The fear of the Lord is the beginning of knowledge; but fools despise wisdom and instruction.* Overall, while wisdom leads to thoughtful and constructive outcomes, foolishness results in poor judgment and negative consequences.

Abigal's Wisdom

In the Bible, the story of Abigail is demonstrative of wisdom in action when she intervened to protect her husband Nabal, from King David's wrath. Nabal was a rich man, but he was known for his foolishness and disrespect. In this particular instance, he had refused to provide David and his men with provisions, despite the fact that David had previously protected Nabal's shepherds, as explained in 1 Samuel 25:15-16. This disregard for David's kindness made David so angry that he had made up in his mind to take revenge by killing Nabal and his entire household. Upon learning of David's intentions, Nabal's wife Abigail quickly took action. In an act of wisdom, she gathered a generous supply of food and wine and set out to meet David before he reached her home. She approached him with kindness and humility, displaying the Law of Honor, and acknowledged his status as king. She also expressed her understanding for his anger and took responsibility for her husband's actions and referred to him as a "fool." In her plea to King David, she skillfully appealed to his empathy and morality. She reminded him that avenging himself could lead to regret and unnecessary bloodshed of innocent people.

Abigal effectively shifted David's anger from vengeance and ended up touching his heart. He was moved by her words and acknowledged her wisdom insight. He thanked her for her intervention and told her that she had prevented him from acting foolishly that day. As a result, David spared Nabal's life, but in an ironic turn of events, Nabal ended up dying from Divine judgment. Abigail's wise actions not only saved her husband and her household that day, but it also established her as a significant figure in David's story when she became his wife. Her ability to navigate a potentially deadly situation with wisdom, humility, and grace highlights the power of wisdom in averting disaster and promoting peace.

Absalom's Foolishness

In a stark contrast, there is a story about what happens to someone when wisdom is absent. Absalom was David's son, but he grew bitter towards his father because he felt that David did not do enough when he learned that his own daughter Tamar had been raped by her own half-brother Amnon, one of David's sons. Absalom was infuriated over the rape of his sister, and he avenged her honor by taking the life of her rapist, who happened to be his brother and David's son. In an attempt to subvert his father's kingdom, Absalom planned to steal the throne from this father and become the King himself. When he faced the threat of David's forces, he had the opportunity to receive wise counsel from Hushai the Archite, who had been one of David's loyal advisors, but Absalom chose to ignore Hushai's wisdom and follow the counsel of one of his childhood friends, Ahithophel instead. Ahithophel's counsel was foolishness. This foolish advice of his friend ultimately led to disastrous consequences. Absalom's failure to

> *"While common sense can guide basic decision-making, true wisdom involves a more reflective and comprehensive approach to understanding life's complexities."*

recognize and act upon true wisdom demonstrated how pride, foolishness, and the desire for immediate gratification (stealing the throne) can cloud judgment and lead to ruin. Absalom's foolishness ultimately led to his downfall and death. This story underscores the path that foolishness can take you on. Being a fool can lead to death and destruction. Choosing foolishness never results in a positive outcome. Godly wisdom is a gift available to all who ask, seek and search for it. It is acquired overtime and through one wise decision after the next. Gaining wisdom can be achieved through prayer, reading and meditating on the Word of God and asking for guidance and understanding. Engaging with scripture is essential because studying the Bible provides insight into God's character and His teachings. Practicing humility, listening to the Holy Spirit, and applying biblical teachings in daily life are also crucial steps in developing Godly wisdom. *Wisdom is the principle thing, therefore get wisdom and in all thy getting, get understanding* (Proverbs 4:7).

Lessons to Live By:

- God's wisdom is the ultimate wisdom because it is a revelation of things not known, but guides, protects and produces understanding and deep insight.

- Wisdom is a Divine gift that is available to all who ask and search for it. It is rooted in a deep understanding of God's statutes and in a relationship with Him.

- While worldly wisdom is definitely valuable and has its place, it is limited and fallible.

- Foolishness is often associated with moral failure and a disregard for God's guidance.

- Acquiring Godly wisdom involves seeking a deeper relationship with God and aligning your life with His principles.

6

Authenticity & Manipulation

Authenticity speaks with honesty and integrity, building trust and true connection, while manipulation deceives, distorting reality for personal gain. Choosing authenticity fosters genuine relationships, while manipulation erodes trust and leaves a hollow legacy.

Becoming authentic is a journey of self-discovery and self-acceptance. It requires intentional reflection and a willingness to align your actions with your true beliefs and values. Discovering oneself on the road to authenticity is a deeply introspective process that unfolds over time, involving awareness, exploration, and acceptance. This journey helps uncover who you are at your core and goes beyond external influences and past conditioning. A person discovers their true self by turning inward. This journey involves noticing what genuinely resonates, exploring passions, and paying attention to inner instincts that reveal core values. By examining deeply ingrained beliefs and societal expectations, a person can let go of imposter identities and align with their true nature. Self-acceptance, which includes embracing your strengths and working on your weaknesses is essential to being authentic. The road to authenticity is a journey of courage that embraces one's genuine nature without fear or the need for external validation.

Authenticity is a different kind of virtue that encompasses emotional awareness, deep thought, character, integrity, humility, and a deep understanding of Divine laws. It begins with self-discovery and embodies the courage to embrace one's true nature, personality, and character traits. Authenticity fosters honesty and transparency in both personal and interpersonal contexts. When individuals live authentically, they cultivate trust and respect in their relationships, as they communicate openly and align their actions with their beliefs. This commitment to being an authentic person strengthens one's character and promotes genuine connections, empowering others to express their true selves as well. Being authentic requires the courage to embrace one's true nature, even when they don't align with external expectations. Authenticity is to live without pretense and to work at being honest and genuine, presenting yourself as who you truly are rather than conforming to how the world thinks you should be. More often than not, an authentic person is self-aware, clear about their values, and acts consistently within those boundaries. This leads to genuine interactions and meaningful connections with others. Past experiences, especially tests and trials, can significantly lead to self-discovery, as challenges often reveal our true strengths, values, and areas for growth. Facing adversity compels introspection, pushing us to confront core beliefs and build resilience. This deepens self-awareness. As we go through these experiences, we prioritize what genuinely matters while shedding superficial layers and aligning more closely with our authentic selves. The trials that we go through can be transformative and can help us embrace our true nature and live with greater integrity and purpose. Authentic people connect more with others because they radiate genuine trustworthiness. Their honesty and openness foster a sense of comfort and safety, which encourages others to be themselves as well.

Authenticity knocks down barriers because people are able to perceive the genuine nature of an authentic person, which gives them the impetus to be their authentic self as well. By aligning their actions and words with their true values, authentic people naturally attract those who appreciate that level of sincerity. This fosters connections that are both impactful and lasting. Being authentic is easier than putting on masks because it requires less mental energy and emotional strain. Authentic people don't have to constantly monitor or adjust their behavior to fit different roles or expectations, which can be draining. This consistency reduces stress and brings inner peace because there's no need to maintain facades. Over time, authenticity becomes freeing, making interactions more natural and allowing for deeper, genuine connections. Living in alignment with your values and being true to yourself reduces feelings of anxiety or guilt that can come from trying to maintain façades. This inner peace and self-acceptance promote relaxation, leading to more restful sleep.

The Samaritan Woman at the Well

The story of the Samaritan woman at the well, found in John 4:7-26, beautifully illustrates the power of authenticity, personal transformation, and connection. When Jesus encounters the woman, he engages her in conversation despite cultural and societal norms that discouraged such interactions between Jews and Samaritans. The Jews conducted themselves as superior to the Samaritans and looked down on them as a lower, less class of Jews. The woman at the well initially went to the well with a sense of internal shame for having lived a life marked by multiple relationships and societal rejection. As their conversation unfolded, she demonstrated authenticity by openly discussing her past and current struggles. When Jesus revealed intimate knowledge of her life, she didn't shy away or attempt to hide her reality; rather, she engaged honestly while recognizing the truth about her life in His words. This moment of vulnerability lead to a profound revelation, as Jesus identified Himself as the Messiah.

The overarching point of authenticity in this story is that true connection and transformation often occurs when we are willing to be open and honest about ourselves, our experiences and our feelings. The woman's willingness to share her life story not only led to her own spiritual awakening but also empowered her to become an evangelist in her community as she shared her encounter with Jesus and encouraged many to seek Him out. Her authenticity not only changed her life but impacted the lives of others, demonstrating that embracing one's true self can lead to life-changing blessings and the ability to connect deeply with others.

Manipulation

In contrast, manipulation comes from a lack of authenticity and can be driven by insecurity or the desire to control outcomes. Those who manipulate tend to disguise their true intentions, which leads to mistrust and superficial interactions. Manipulation is a psychological strategy used to influence or control the thoughts, feelings, or actions of others for personal gain. It usually involves deceit, coercion, psychological games, or underhanded tactics, ostensibly masking the manipulator's true intentions to achieve desired outcomes. Some people manipulate, but they do not even realize they do it because it has become a habit for them and they do it so frequently. Manipulation can stem from various sources, including insecurity, fear of rejection, a desire for power, or a need to avoid vulnerability. It may arise in interpersonal relationships, workplaces, or social dynamics, reflecting an imbalance of power where one person or entity seeks to exploit the weaknesses or emotions of another.

Manipulation is definitely a vice because it involves deceit, a desire to control and a lack of transparency. It undermines trust and can destroy genuine relationships. Manipulation typically prioritizes the manipulator's desires over the well-being and feelings of others, leading to ethical violations or emotional harm. Manipulation can erode communication, create imbalances of power, and cause resentment. This weakens the foundation of respect and honesty that healthy relationships require. Additionally, manipulation has an element that is willing to exploit the vulnerabilities of others in an effort to expose a deficiency in character. Ultimately, manipulation detracts from authentic interactions and promotes a culture of mistrust and disconnection. This vice works hand in hand with deceit, as it often involves misleading others to achieve personal goals. It is characteristic of deceitfulness, lack of transparency, and emotional exploitation that relies on lies or half-truths to achieve one's goals. Ultimately, the reliance on manipulation can create a cycle of negative behaviors, further entrenching people in a web of moral and ethical vices.

One can be manipulative without realizing it, often due to unconscious habits or unexamined motivations. They might act in ways to achieve desired outcomes, using subtle influences or persuasion that feels natural to them but impacts the choices of others. This can stem from insecurity, a need for control, or learned behaviors, where they may genuinely believe they are helping rather than manipulating. Without self-awareness, manipulators might not see how their actions affect others. When you bring their manipulative ways to their attention, they may respond defensively or with denial since admitting manipulation can threaten their perceived strength and self-image. Some manipulators might rationalize their behaviors, and claim that their intentions are good, or they may shift blame, saying that others "misunderstand" them. When they humbly reflect and admit that their ways are, can be, or have been manipulative, they might feel embarrassment or guilt and become open to change. This can be the insightful moment when they become self-aware. However, if they are unwilling to acknowledge their behavior, they may deflect or continue with similar manipulative tactics.

For a manipulative person to be delivered from this vice, they need to have a genuine desire to change. This is predicated upon self-awareness and humility. Recognizing the negative impact of their actions on others is essential, as it helps shift their perspective from self-centered motives to empathy and consideration for the feelings of others. This change requires ongoing reflection, accountability, and sometimes guidance from trusted friends, mentors or counselors. Developing integrity, practicing open communication, and focusing on authentic connections can gradually replace manipulative tendencies, fostering healthier, more genuine relationships. Ultimately, true transformation comes from consistent effort, self-discipline, and a commitment to personal growth.

The Serpent's Manipulation

Manipulation entered the world through the deception of the serpent in the Garden of Eden. In the book of Genesis, the serpent used manipulation to deceive Eve by questioning God's command regarding the forbidden fruit. He implied that God was withholding knowledge and that eating the fruit would lead to their enlightenment. This manipulation created doubt in Eve's mind about God's intentions. When she chose to eat the fruit and then gave it to Adam, both willfully acted against God's direct command. As a result of their disobedience, they were punished and were expelled from the garden. This symbolized the loss of innocence, but more devastating was that it introduced sin into the world. Their punishment stemmed from their choice to trust the serpent's manipulation over God's Word, highlighting the consequences of disobedience and the breach of the Divine command, which led to a devastating and far-reaching negative impact in the world.

It is important to avoid being manipulated in order to protect your self-sufficiency, maintain self-respect, and make decisions that are aligned with your values. To navigate away from manipulators, you must set clear boundaries, trust your instincts, and remain firm in your convictions. Stay aware of emotional triggers that manipulators like to use in order to exploit and upset you. When communicating, do so assertively and seek support of trusted counselors, therapists, mentors, friends or spiritual leaders if needed. Recognizing manipulation and refusing to engage disarms the manipulator's tactics. This allows you to maintain control over your choices and well-being.

Embracing authenticity is essential for personal growth, building and maintaining fulfilling relationships, and overall well-being. When people make every effort to be authentic, they cultivate a genuine sense of self that fosters confidence and self-acceptance. By living authentically, we also model integrity while inspiring those around us to embrace their true selves as well. Embracing authenticity not only enriches our own lives but also creates a ripple effect of sincerity and trustworthiness in the world, highlighting the transformative power of being true to oneself in a complex and often deceptive landscape. This opens the door to a life of true fulfillment and genuine connection. When you choose to live your life aligned with your values and express your unique self, you cultivate inner peace and build trust with those around you. Step into the freedom that comes with authenticity, knowing that by being true to yourself, you inspire others to do the same.

Lessons to Live By:

- A person discovers their true self by engaging in a process of deep self-awareness by turning inward. This journey involves noticing what genuinely resonates, exploring passions, and paying attention to inner instincts that reveal core values.

- Authenticity is to live without pretense. It involves being honest and genuine, presenting yourself as you are rather than conforming to how the world thinks you should be.

- Manipulation typically prioritizes the manipulator's desires over the well-being and feelings of others, leading to ethical violations and emotional harm.

- One can be manipulative without realizing it, often due to unconscious habits or unexamined motivations.

- For a manipulative person to be delivered from this vice, they need to have a genuine desire to change. This is rooted in self-awareness and humility.

7

Trust & Doubt

Trust anchors the soul in certainty, while doubt creates unrest. Trust allows us to rest in assurance, seeing beyond obstacles, while doubt clouds our vision, making the journey ahead unsteady and the heart unsettled.

Trust and doubt are two opposing forces that shape our spiritual journeys and influence how we navigate the challenges of life. Trust is a confident belief in God's reliability and the assurance that He is always working things out for our good, even when circumstances seem bleak. Trust enables us to surrender our doubts, worries and fears to God, while acknowledging His sovereignty and wisdom in every situation. It is cultivated through prayer, worship, and the continuous study of scripture. Trust strengthens a relationship with God founded in love, dependence, and obedience. It is the firm belief in the reliability, truth, Divinity, and strength of God and His promises. It involves a surrender of all to Him - our worries, doubt, and fears. Trust is rooted in faith and belief and reflects a relationship that is built on love, dependence, and obedience. As Christians, we are called to trust God, even in difficult times, believing that He works "all" things for our good (Romans 8:28). This trust is often expressed through prayer, worship, and reliance on scripture. Trust in God is demonstrated through practices and attitudes that reflect faith and reliance in Him and on Him. The difference between faith "in" God and faith "on" God lies primarily in the focus and application of said faith. Faith "in" God refers to a deep, personal belief and trust in His character, promises, and existence. It entails a relational aspect, where we place our confidence in who God is and His ability to fulfill His Word. In contrast, faith "on" God implies a reliance on His power and provisions in specific situations, emphasizing action and dependence. It suggests actively leaning on Him for support, guidance, and intervention in life's circumstances. While both terms convey trust and belief, faith "in" God emphasizes the relationship and trust in His nature, while faith "on" God highlights reliance on Him in practical, everyday situations.

Trust is a virtue because it fosters positive relationships and strengthens bonds. You cannot have faith without trust. As a foundational element in relationships, trust encourages open communication, freedom to be oneself, and mutual respect, allowing people to connect more deeply. Trust reflects qualities such as integrity, reliability, and honesty, which are essential for building strong, healthy interactions. When trust is present, people are more likely to engage in supportive behaviors and work towards common goals. Thus, trust is seen as a virtue that nurtures a sense of security and cultivates a spirit of compassion and understanding among individuals.

Distrust and Doubt

The opposite of trust is distrust and doubt. While distrust refers to a lack of confidence in someone's reliability or intentions, doubt encompasses a broader uncertainty or skepticism regarding beliefs or convictions, including questions about God's existence or promises. Doubt can lead to hesitation in placing trust in relationships or in God, creating barriers to faith and reliance. While distrust often pertains to specific individuals or situations, doubt can arise from internal struggles, external circumstances, or conflicting information, affecting one's overall belief system. Thus, while distrust is a form of doubt related to specific trust issues, doubt itself serves as a broader concept that reflects uncertainty in faith and trust overall. Doubt leads to feelings of insecurity and uncertainty in a relationship, causing individuals to question the motives behind one's actions and words. Doubt is the opposite of trust because while trust fosters a sense of safety, openness, and connection, distrust breeds suspicion, fear, and withdrawal. For example, in a relationship characterized by distrust, communication often breaks down, as individuals may withhold their thoughts and feelings, fearing betrayal, rejection or misunderstanding. This can result in defensiveness, conflict, and a lack of emotional intimacy. Distrust can manifest as a reluctance to rely on or support someone. This undermines the foundation necessary for a healthy, functioning relationship. As a result, while trust encourages growth and collaboration, distrust hinders development and can lead to the eventual deterioration of relationships.

Doubt and Distrust as Vices

Doubt and distrust are vices because they undermine relationships, hinder personal growth, and foster negativity. Distrust creates barriers between people, leading to suspicion, conflict, and emotional distance. It can erode the foundation of healthy interactions, preventing open communication and collaboration. Doubt, on the other hand, can paralyze decision-making and diminish one's ability to take risks or embrace opportunities. Doubt often leads to fear, anxiety, and a lack of confidence, which can stifle faith and hinder spiritual or personal development. Both distrust and doubt can foster a mindset focused on negativity and uncertainty, making it difficult for individuals to build strong connections or maintain a positive outlook. As a result, these attitudes can lead to isolation, bitterness, and a reluctance to trust others or engage fully in life, making them detrimental to overall well-being and community cohesion.

Abraham's Trust

Abraham's trust in God was profoundly illustrated when he was commanded to sacrifice his only son, Isaac. Despite the turmoil and sadness that filled his heart, Abraham did not hesitate to obey. His willingness to

> *"Trust in God is demonstrated through practices and attitudes that reflect faith and reliance in Him and on Him."*

follow God's directive, even in such a heart-wrenching situation, demonstrated remarkable trust in God. Abraham's obedience was demonstrated when he prepared to carry out the sacrifice until God intervened, providing a ram as a substitute. This act exemplified Abraham's great trust in God, showing that he believed in God's goodness and promise, even amid immense personal sacrifice and anguish.

Zachariah's Doubt

Zachariah was the biological father of John the Baptist. His doubt was revealed when the angel Gabriel announced that he would have a son, despite how old both he and his wife, Elizabeth were. Unlike Abraham, who responded to God's command with unwavering trust, Zachariah questioned the angel's message, expressing skepticism about the possibility of such a miracle. As a consequence of his doubt, Zachariah became mute until the prophecy was fulfilled, showing the consequences that come with disbelief. In contrast, Abraham's trust led to the fulfillment of God's promises, resulting in the birth of Isaac and the establishment of a covenant with God. Abraham's faith brought blessings, while Zachariah's doubt led to a period of silence and self-reflection. This contrast underscores the rewards of trust and the consequences of doubt in a person's relationship with God. To strengthen trust in various areas of your life, consider the following advice:

1. **Practice Open Communication**: Engage in honest and transparent conversations. Share your thoughts and feelings and encourage others to do the same. Doing this can build understanding and clarity.

2. **Set Boundaries**: Establish clear boundaries to protect yourself while fostering trust. Communicating your limits can create a safe space for both parties.

3. **Be Authentic**: Embrace your true self by understanding your values and beliefs. Communicate openly and honestly, share your feelings, and don't be afraid to show vulnerability. Express your individuality and don't become someone you are not for the sake of "fitting in."

4. **Reflect on Past Experiences**: Assess previous relationships and situations. Identify patterns of trust or distrust and consider what you can learn from those experiences to improve future interactions.

5. **Give Trust Gradually**: Start by trusting people in small ways and gradually increase your level of trust as they prove themselves reliable. This can help reduce the fear of betrayal.

6. **Practice Forgiveness**: Understand that mistakes happen. Being willing to forgive can help you move past grievances and rebuild trust.

7. **Cultivate a Positive Mindset**: Focus on the good in others and seek to understand their intentions. A positive outlook can help you approach relationships with an open heart.

8. **Develop Emotional Awareness**: Be mindful of your emotions and how they affect your perceptions of others. Recognizing your feelings can help you respond more constructively in challenging situations.

By applying these strategies, you can create an atmosphere of trust and foster stronger and more meaningful relationships with others. Trust and doubt play pivotal roles in shaping our spiritual lives and the quality of our relationships. Trust in God is the foundation upon which we build our faith, and through this trust, we experience His faithfulness and the blessings that follow. As demonstrated in the stories of Abraham and Zachariah, trust brings reward and fulfillment, while doubt often leads to consequences that hinder growth and spiritual progress. Cultivating trust, both in God and in our relationships with others, requires intentional effort and self-discipline. It is through open communication, authenticity, forgiveness, and a positive mindset that we nurture the virtue of trust, while overcoming the vices of doubt and distrust. By doing so, we can experience greater peace, deeper connections, and a life marked by unwavering faith in God's provision and goodness.

Lessons to Live By:

- Trust is rooted in faith and belief and reflects a relationship that is built on love, dependence, and obedience.

- Trust is a virtue because it fosters positive relationships and strengthens bonds.

- Doubt can lead to hesitation in placing trust in relationships or in God, creating barriers to faith and reliance.

- Doubt and distrust are considered vices because they undermine relationships, hinder personal growth, and foster negativity.

- As Christians, we are called to trust God, even in difficult times, believing that He works "all" things for our good (Romans 8:28).

8

Holiness & Sin

Holiness reflects a life aligned with God's will and brings purity and purpose, while sin separates and leads to brokenness and despair. Choosing holiness draws us closer to Divine truth, while sin distances us from eternal peace.

As a virtue, holiness is a state of being set apart and dedicated to God's purpose. It reflects the very essence of God's nature. Holiness goes beyond just rule-following, but it cultivates a sincere heart that seeks closeness with God and strives to reflect His goodness. This leads to an inner purity that shapes one's thoughts, words, and actions and promotes a life of peace, kindness, and righteousness. In Scripture, holiness is God's perfection, righteousness, and moral purity, highlighting a separation from sin. For believers, holiness involves living in a way that aligns to God's character and striving to foster virtues such as love, kindness, humility, and obedience to His Word. Holiness is not about how one looks or acts but has to do with a heart that is truly devoted to God, one that seeks to honor Him in thoughts, intentions, and actions. When we say that God "sits in His holiness," it demonstrates both His absolute purity and also His sovereignty. God's holiness is not just a characteristic but is the epitome of who He is. This makes him completely separate from sin, darkness, and anything contrary to His nature. "Sitting" in His holiness suggests that He reigns from a place of perfect moral integrity and righteousness. To "sit" also implies His authority and judgment, as the ultimate Judge who, from His holy throne, discerns right from wrong. His Holiness is the foundation from which He governs and where He extends mercy, justice, and truth. He is both the source and standard of holiness, ruling from a place of pure, incorruptible goodness, and calling His people to reflect that same holiness in their lives.

As Christians, we exemplify holiness in our lives by striving to align our actions, thoughts, and attitudes to God's nature. This involves a sincere commitment to living according to His standards and a daily effort to separate ourselves from sin while seeking purity in heart and behavior. When some hear the word "holiness" they think of long skirts, no makeup, plain looking men and women who are nerds. They think of people who don't go to parties and don't have fun; but holiness simply has to do with living lives set apart for God while striving to reflect God's character in all we do. You can still have fun while being holy. You can still wear makeup, go to parties and have a good time. Holiness simply means that you refuse to engage in any activity that does not reflect God's nature and that you are always cognizant that God is watching. Laughing, joking, dancing, singing, playing games and having fun does not mean that you are not holy. There is purity in all of those things. Can they be taken too far, yes! But holiness allows you to know just how far to go and what boundaries not to cross. Holiness seeks to embody values such as honesty, humility, and integrity and consciously avoids sinful behaviors. As Christians, our aim should be to influence the world around us while shining as lights that point others toward God. Holiness is a daily commitment and a journey of spiritual growth, marked by continuous surrender to God and reliance on His grace to live a life that honors Him.

Holiness is profoundly contrary from the world's standards because it is rooted in God's unchanging nature, while worldly standards often shift with cultural trends, social constructs, personal preferences, or societal values. Worldly standards prioritize self-interests, material gains, power, control, position and individual freedom over spiritual or moral accountability. Worldly standards often focus on achievements, appearances, and personal happiness, which can sometimes lead to compromising one's integrity for convenience or success. Holiness, however, emphasizes internal transformation and integrity that seeks to honor God in all things, even if it means sacrificing comfort, popularity, or success. While the world may condone or even celebrate behaviors that are self-centered or morally ambiguous, holiness calls Christians to a life of selflessness, truthfulness, and love, adhering to a higher standard. This distinction often places us at odds with popular culture, but it also offers a distinctive witness that demonstrates the peace, purpose, and fulfillment that come from living a life dedicated to God.

King Josiah's Righteousness

King Josiah of Judah was the son of Amon and the grandson of Manasseh, both of whom led the nation of Israel into deep idolatry and sin. Josiah ascended to the throne at only eight years old after his father Amon was assassinated by his own servants. Josiah's early years were marked by spiritual darkness in Judah because of the previous kings who had done egregious things that displeased God. His grandfather and father had led the nation into deep sin. They had built altars to pagan gods across the land, filled the land with idols, practiced witchcraft, did morally corrupt rituals and even sacrificed children. They even did sorcery and consulted mediums, which were all abominations according to God's law. This caused a deep spiritual decline and moral decay in Judah. Despite his lineage, Josiah was different. By the age of sixteen, he began earnestly seeking God for guidance, following the example of his ancestor King David.

A pivotal moment in Josiah's reign came during the repair of the temple, when the Book of the Law was found. Hearing the Scriptures for the first time, he was overwhelmed with grief over Judah's sins. When he turned twenty years old or so, he began major changes to remove idol worship from Judah. He ordered the destruction of all of the pagan altars and high places, and he renewed the covenant between God and the people by leading them in a public recommitment to follow God's laws. After the Book of the Law was discovered during the temple repairs, Josiah gathered all the people of Judah, including the elders, priests, and citizens, to the temple. He read the words of the law out loud and emphasized everyone's responsibility to obey God. Josiah then pledged to follow the covenant wholeheartedly and encouraged the people to do the same. He reaffirmed their commitment to worship only God, get rid of all idols and false gods and obey His commandments (2 Kings 23:1-3; 2 Chronicles 34:29-32). His dedication to God's holiness distinguished him as one of Judah's most faithful kings because he brought temporary spiritual revival and peace to the nation. God considered Josiah holy because of his sincere repentance, zeal for righteousness, and his efforts to lead Judah back to faithful worship. In response, God blessed him by granting peace during his reign and spared him from witnessing Judah's impending judgment, affirming His pleasure in Josiah's faithfulness.

Sin

The dichotomy between sin and holiness is at the heart of the Christian journey. Sin is any thought, action, or attitude that goes against God's commands and character. In essence, sin is a moral and spiritual failing that separates us from God's holiness and deviates us from His will and the purpose He has for humanity. Sin often involves choosing selfish desires, pleasures, pride, or rebellion over obedience and submission to God's guidance. Sin can be described as "missing the mark," like a ship navigating without a compass, straying from its intended destination and heading into danger. This symbolizes falling short of God's standard of righteousness. Sin is essentially disobedience to God. Sin is designed to contaminate, corrupt and engage in everything contrary to the will of God. Sin opposes holiness because it disrupts the purity and alignment with God's will that holiness represents. Holiness calls people to a higher and pure way of living, marked by integrity, values, standards, and a focus on eternal life. Sin calls people into degradation, moral corruptness, darkness and depravity.

As previously discussed, sin entered the world through the disobedience of Adam and Eve in the Garden of Eden, as described in the book of Genesis. God had commanded them not to eat from the tree of the knowledge of good and evil. However, they allowed themselves to get deceived by the serpent and chose to disregard God's directive. This act of disobedience was known as "The Fall" and introduced sin into the human experience. This one act of disobedience corrupted and destroyed the perfect harmony and purity that God had created. It led to spiritual separation from God by breaking the perfect relationship that humans had with Him because sin cannot coexist with God's holiness. When Adam and Eve disobeyed God, they chose their own will over His instructions thus, introducing sin, rebellion and distrust into the world. As a result, humanity became separated from God's presence which led to a spiritual void that only God's forgiveness and redemption could restore. This separation affected all people and created a need for reconciliation with God. Adam and Eve's sin continues to reverberate in the world today through various forms: disobedience, lying, stealing, murder, adultery, greed, hate, envy, and so much more. Sin harms both the sinner and those around them.

Sin disrupts the harmony that God intended in relationships, which leads to guilt, shame, and spiritual consequences. From a Christian perspective, sin is serious because not only does it damage our relationship with God, but it hinders spiritual growth. However, through Jesus' sacrifice, sin can be forgiven and overcome, allowing for reconciliation with God and the pursuit of a holy and transformed life. When sin came, it brought disease, physical suffering, infirmities and death, which were not part of God's initial design. Sin disrupted the original, perfect order that God had created. This curse on humanity and creation led to physical ailments, aging, and environmental challenges that all people face. Sin's impact on the body and the world is a reminder of the separation from God's life-sustaining presence.

While holiness seeks to honor and emulate God's goodness, righteousness and purity, sin indulges in selfish desires, pride, and rebellion often focusing on the lust of the eyes, the lust of the flesh and the pride of life. Where holiness fosters closeness to God, unity with others, and peace, sin brings spiritual disconnection, harm to relationships, and inner turmoil. Holiness promotes purity, love, and humility, sin leads to impurity, hatred, and arrogance. Sin leads us away from God's order and purpose, while holiness seeks to embody and reflect God's will. The entry of sin led to the degradation of humanity and the world in several ways:

1. **Spiritual Separation from God**: Sin broke the intimate relationship humans once had with God. This separation caused a spiritual void and has led to widespread idolatry, disbelief, and a loss of Divine purpose and fulfillment.

2. **Moral Decay**: Sin has led to a world where selfishness, greed, hatred, murder, crime and violence are pervasive. These behaviors have eroded societies, families, and personal relationships, often resulting in pain, injustice, and oppression.

3. **Physical Suffering and Death**: Sin brought mortality and physical suffering into the world, impacting health, nature, and the environment. As a result, humanity now experiences disease, natural disasters, and aging, which were not part of God's original design.

4. **Environmental Degradation**: Human sinfulness, such as greed and disregard for stewardship, has led to environmental destruction, exploitation of natural resources, and pollution, affecting ecosystems and causing suffering across all forms of life.

In essence, sin has distorted every aspect of creation, replacing God's original order with disorder. It perpetuates cycles of brokenness, causing individuals and societies to suffer from the consequences of actions and attitudes contrary to God's holiness.

Achan's Sin

The story of Achan is found in the book of Joshua, chapters 6 and 7, during Israel's conquest of the Promised Land. After the walls of Jericho miraculously fell down, God commanded the Israelites to destroy everything in the city as an offering to Him. He warned them not to take anything for themselves. However, some of the most valuable items such as gold, silver, and fine clothing, were to be placed in the Lord's treasury. Israel's success in battle depended on their strict obedience to God's directives. Achan was an Israelite soldier. After conquering the city of Jericho, he saw a beautiful Babylonian robe among the ruins that he wanted for himself. The robe was silver and gold. He also took 200 shekels of silver and a wedge of gold. This was against God's command, but Achan, knowing this still stole them and hid them in his tent, hoping to keep this his secret, not realizing that the eyes of the Lord are in every place. His sin wasn't just theft but also direct disobedience to God that violated the covenant. Achan's actions were driven by greed and a lack of faith because he saw the valuables as an opportunity for personal gain. He chose to trust in material wealth over God's provision and disregarded the Divine instructions meant to protect Israel. After Achan did this, Israel went to battle against the smaller town of Ai, expecting an easy victory. However, they were unexpectedly defeated and loss 36 soldiers in that battle. Joshua was very distressed and began to pray to God about why they lost that battle.

God revealed to Joshua that Israel had sinned by taking forbidden items. To identify the culprit, Joshua gathered each tribe and through a process of casting lots, God led Joshua to Achan's tribe, clan, family, and finally to Achan himself. When Achan was confronted by Joshua, he confessed his sin. As punishment for his disobedience, Achan, along with his whole family, was taken to the Valley of Achor. There, they were stoned, and all of his possessions were burned. This severe judgment was intended to demonstrate the seriousness of sin, especially when it affects the entire community's relationship with God. Afterward, God's anger relented, and Israel regained His favor, allowing them to conquer Ai and continue their journey to the Promised Land. Achan's story is a sobering reminder of how individual sin does not only affect us, but can bring harm to others as well. It emphasizes how we must consider the overall and far-reaching cost of sinning, realizing that engaging in it will not only jeopardize our own livelihood and spiritual standing, but our personal sins can also affect those closest to us to the point of death! Sin does not only affect the one committing it, but can have broader impacts on families, communities, and even societies. This story highlights the importance of obedience, integrity and responsibility in faith. Personal sin creates consequences that ripple outward, influencing relationships, trust, and the well-being of others.

Remaining holy in a world that values personal freedom and subjective "truth" requires a conscious commitment to God's values over society's shifting standards. This path often involves making difficult choices to prioritize God's Word over popular opinion, even when it means facing misunderstanding or opposition.

Lessons to Live By:

- Holiness is a state of being set apart and dedicated to God's purpose. It reflects the very essence of God's nature.

- Holiness is profoundly contrary from the world's standards because it is rooted in God's unchanging nature, while worldly standards often shift with cultural trends, social constructs, personal preferences, or societal values.

- Sin is essentially disobedience to God and the dichotomy between sin and holiness is at the heart of the Christian journey.

- Sin disrupts the harmony that God intended in relationships, which leads to guilt, shame, and spiritual consequences.

- Remaining holy in a world that values personal freedom and subjective "truth" requires a conscious commitment to God's values over society's shifting standards.

9

Self-discipline & Procrastination

Self-discipline drives purposeful action and builds momentum towards goals, while procrastination delays progress and leads to missed opportunities.

Self-discipline and procrastination are two contrasting habits that significantly determine the trajectory and achievements in our lives. Self-discipline is at the heart of personal development and contains attributes of self-control, perseverance, resilience and a commitment to long-term goals. It empowers us to prioritize our values and aspirations, while guiding us to make choices that align with our true selves, even amidst the distractions and temptations that life presents. By practicing self-discipline, we learn to resist the allure of short-term gratification and pave the way for more meaningful and lasting rewards. The virtue of self-discipline embodies qualities such as control, perseverance, and commitment to long-term goals. Moreover, it fosters responsibility and allows us to manage our time and resources effectively. It also cultivates resilience and gives us the strength to overcome obstacles while remaining focused on our goals despite challenges. Self-discipline encourages us to act with intention and purpose and creates a foundation for achieving personal and professional fulfillment. This attribute reflects a commitment to bettering oneself and is essential for navigating life's vicissitudes while maintaining our integrity and focus.

This particular virtue also assists in helping to control impulses and emotions. It is displayed in one's life through consistent actions, such as setting and adhering to routines, managing time effectively, and resisting temptations that can distract you from your objectives. Those with self-discipline prioritize their commitments, work diligently toward their ambitions and pursuits, and maintain focus despite challenges. Cultivating self-discipline is a worthy undertaking because it allows a person to grow personally while fostering resilience and success. It gives the ability to overcome obstacles, develop healthy habits, and achieve goals, ultimately leading to a more fulfilling and purposeful life.

Someone who is self-disciplined typically demonstrates consistency, focus, self-awareness, and the ability to set and achieve goals. They effectively manage their time, prioritize their responsibilities and resist temptations. In contrast, a person with little to no self-discipline may struggle with impulsivity and difficulty maintaining commitments. This often results in missed opportunities, unfulfilled goals, and a sense of frustration or lack of control over their life. These are those who are always late, turn things in at the last minute and expect others to drop what they are doing to assist them. Ultimately, self-discipline fosters personal growth and accomplishment, while its absence can lead to stagnation and dissatisfaction.

Procrastination

Procrastination is the opposite of self-discipline because it is the act of delaying or postponing tasks or decisions, often in favor of more enjoyable, comfortable or less challenging activities. It is characterized by a tendency to delay or avoid responsibilities then trying to get them done at the final hour, which leads to a diminished quality or last minute results. Trying to get things done at the 11th hour leads to feelings of frustration, stress, and anxiety as deadlines approach. Procrastination can hinder productivity and prevent you from achieving your goals, resulting in a cycle of avoidance and decreased self-efficacy. Procrastination is considered a vice because it reflects a lack of prioritizing, discipline and self-control leading to negative consequences in many aspects of life. Procrastination often hinders personal and professional growth and prevents people from reaching their full potential and achieving their goals. This not only affects productivity but also undermines overall well-being and self-esteem, making it a detrimental behavior that contradicts the virtues of diligence and self-discipline. Chronic procrastination can lead to a cycle of avoidance, making it harder to tackle tasks in the future and reinforces negative habits. Overall, the cumulative effects of procrastination can hinder success, well-being, and overall life satisfaction.

The Procrastinating Virgins

In the Parable of the Ten Virgins, the story unfolds in the context of a wedding celebration, where the virgins are waiting for the arrival of the bridegroom to join the festivities. This event was a significant occasion in their culture, marked by joy and elation. However, procrastination greatly affected the foolish virgins, who neglected to prepare for the bridegroom's arrival by not putting oil in their lamps. By failing to do this, they found themselves unprepared when the moment finally came. As the bridegroom approached, their lamps were low, so they could not light or see their way to the wedding feast. This lack of preparation resulted in their exclusion from the celebration and forced them to miss out on the joy and blessings of the occasion. Their procrastination cost them dearly, serving as a cautionary tale about the importance of not procrastinating and being ready for important moments in life. In contrast, the wise virgins demonstrated self-discipline by planning ahead and ensuring they had sufficient oil in their lamps far in advance. Their preparedness allowed them to greet the bridegroom and enter the feast, receiving the blessing of being part of the joyful occasion. This contrast highlights how self-discipline leads to readiness and rewards, while procrastination can result in missed opportunities and regret.

From a spiritual context, the bridegroom symbolizes Jesus Christ and His anticipated return. The bridegroom's arrival is crucial because it signifies the

> *"Those with self-discipline prioritize their commitments, work diligently toward their ambitions and pursuits, and maintain focus despite challenges."*

start of the wedding feast, a metaphor for the ultimate union between Christ and His followers. In the cultural context of the parable, the bridegroom would typically come to take his bride to his home, marking the beginning of their married life together. While the virgins themselves were not to marry the bridegroom in the parable, they served as guests or companions to the bride, thus playing a vital role in the celebration. Their preparedness for the bridegroom's arrival reflects the importance of being spiritually ready for Christ's return, emphasizing vigilance, readiness, and the significance of maintaining a faithful relationship with God. The parable illustrated the consequences of procrastinating and highlights the joy of being welcomed into the eternal celebration with Christ.

Ruth's Remarkable Self-discipline

The story of Ruth exemplifies remarkable self-discipline and dedication, particularly in her commitment to care for her mother-in-law, Naomi. After the death of their husbands, Ruth chose to stay with Naomi thus, demonstrating her loyalty and strong resolve. Each day, she rose up early to work in the fields to gather grains in order to provide for both of them. She toiled from sunrise to sunset in those fields and displayed an unwavering work ethic that reflected her determination to support her mother-in-law and ensure their survival. Ruth's self-discipline was evident not only in her consistent efforts but also in the spirit of excellence she brought to her work. Her diligence did not go unnoticed either. Others recognized her hard work and diligence, as well as her positive attitude. This attracted the attention of Boaz, the owner of the fields, who admired her character, integrity and work ethic. In the end, Ruth's self-discipline and perseverance were greatly rewarded when Boaz married her, securing a future for both her and Naomi. Ruth's story underscores how self-discipline, combined with a strong work ethic and a positive spirit, can lead to significant blessings and recognition, ultimately transforming her life and that of her family.

Self-discipline is closely aligned with character because it reflects a person's values, integrity, and ability to make principled decisions. A person with strong self-discipline demonstrates commitment, responsibility, and the willingness to prioritize long-term goals over immediate gratification. This alignment between self-discipline and character produces resilience because those who are disciplined are better equipped to navigating challenges and setbacks with a steady resolve. Working to be self-disciplined requires sacrifice because it involves relinquishing short-term pleasures or leisure for the sake of achieving greater, long-term achievement. By sacrificing comfort or convenience, you can cultivate the habits and routines necessary for self-discipline, ultimately leading to a more fulfilling and purposeful life. The journey to becoming more self-disciplined also enhances one's character by instilling values such as patience, persistence and determination. As you practice self-discipline, you build confidence and a sense of accomplishment, which reinforces your character and integrity. Therefore, investing in self-discipline through sacrifice is essential for personal transformation, fostering not only individual success but also a strong, virtuous character.

Lessons to Live By:

- By exercising self-discipline, people resist short-term gratification in favor of greater, long-lasting rewards. This leads to personal growth and success.

- Procrastination is the opposite of self-discipline because it is the act of delaying or postponing tasks or decisions, often in favor of more enjoyable, comfortable or less challenging activities.

- By sacrificing comfort or convenience, you can cultivate the habits and routines necessary for self-discipline, ultimately leading to a more fulfilling and purposeful life.

- Investing in self-discipline through sacrifice is essential for personal transformation, fostering not only individual success but also a strong, virtuous character.

10

Gratitude & Entitlement

Gratitude embraces blessings with humility, seeing each gift as precious, while entitlement expects without appreciation and breeds discontent. A grateful heart finds joy in abundance, while entitlement blinds us to life's true riches.

Gratitude and entitlement represent two different approaches to life that influences our perspectives and relationships. Gratitude is a heart-centered virtue that encourages one to recognize and appreciate the abundance that life offers. It shifts our focus from what we don't have to the blessings we do have. This practice of embracing gratitude fosters a sense of joy, contentment, and connection to others and inspires us to acknowledge the kindness and support we receive. When we embrace gratitude, we open ourselves up to a cycle of generosity and goodwill that invites more blessings into our lives and strengthens our bonds with those around us. The virtue of gratitude produces a positive outlook on life by encouraging us to look at life from a thankful and appreciative vantage point. This perspective leads to increased happiness and contentment. Gratitude enhances relationships by encouraging individuals to acknowledge and appreciate the kindness and support of others. When people are thankful, they are often motivated to reciprocate kindness, creating a cycle of generosity and giving. Gratitude is a powerful and transformative force. When you are genuinely thankful for even the smallest things, God blesses you with more, and the blessings continue pouring in. Gratitude is an attitude of the heart that recognizes the undeserved blessings and gifts received and expresses appreciation for them. When you practice gratitude, you are choosing to focus on the positive, rather than dwelling on the negative. This helps you to maintain a sense of joy and contentment, even in difficult circumstances. Gratitude is not just a feeling or sentiment, but an active choice. It requires intentionality in your thoughts and actions, and a sincere appreciation for all that you have. By practicing gratitude, you are also building habits of mindfulness and enthusiasm, which help to maintain a healthy perspective on life. Those who are grateful, experience greater satisfaction, unexplained joy, and optimism. Ultimately, gratitude enriches your life and allows you to savor the present moment with joy and appreciation. You have so much to be grateful for!

Gratitude is tied to humility. Recognizing and appreciating the kindness, support, or blessings received from others requires a humble acknowledgment that you are not entirely self-sufficient. Gratitude shifts the focus away from self-centeredness and invites an awareness of how others contribute to your well-being. Expressing gratitude also involves admitting that you have received help or gifts, which can promote a sense of vulnerability. This acknowledgment fosters humility by reminding you of your interdependence. Furthermore, gratitude and humility both encourage a mindset that is open to recognizing the good in your life. When you approach life with humility, you are more inclined to appreciate the small joys and acts of kindness that might otherwise go unnoticed. In essence, gratitude nurtures humility by cultivating a spirit of appreciation, while humility deepens your ability to express gratitude, creating a positive cycle that enhances personal growth and relational connections.

The opposite of gratitude is ingratitude or entitlement. Ingratitude involves a lack of appreciation for the kindness, support, or benefits received from others, leading to feelings of apathy, neglect, or a disregard for what has been done for you. Entitlement reflects a belief that you "deserve" certain privileges or benefits without necessarily earning them or working for them. This mindset is a direct contrast with gratitude, which involves recognizing and valuing the contributions and kindness of others. When someone feels entitled, they may overlook or dismiss any acts of kindness while taking them for granted. In contrast, gratitude promotes appreciation and acknowledgment of the efforts of others and fosters a positive relationship and emotional well-being. While entitlement emphasizes an expectation of receiving without appreciation, gratitude focuses on recognizing and valuing what one has been given, making them fundamentally opposing concepts.

People may show entitlement by expecting special treatment, disregarding rules or norms, making demands without negotiation, or expressing anger or frustration when expectations aren't met. These behaviors can negatively impact relationships and create a disconnection from others, as entitlement often disregards the efforts and contributions of those around them. Entitlement is a vice because it is self-centered and leads people to prioritize their own needs over everyone else's. It creates a lack of gratitude because it overlooks acts of kindness and breeds unrealistic expectations resulting in dissatisfaction and resentment when those expectations are unmet. A person cannot be grateful and entitled at the same time. The two are diametrically opposed. Additionally, entitlement can lead to resistance to accountability, as individuals may refuse to take responsibility for their own actions that create negative circumstances. Overall, entitlement undermines humility and damages relationships, creating negative social dynamics and personal growth barriers.

Hannah's Gratitude

The story of Hannah is found in 1 Samuel 1 and 2 in the Old Testament. Hannah was one of two wives of Elkanah, and she faced emotional turmoil due to her inability to conceive a child. This situation was very distressing in ancient Hebrew culture, where bearing children was highly valued, and being childless brought shame and depression. Hannah's deep longing for a child led her to fervently pray to the Lord. During one of her visits to Shiloh, where the Ark of the Covenant was kept, she made a solemn vow to God. She promised Him that if He granted her a son, she would dedicate him to the service of the Lord for his entire life. This vow demonstrated her desperation. She not only asked for a child, but she was willing to give him back to God. Her prayers were so intense that the priest Eli initially mistook her for being drunk. Her lips were moving, but the words could not be heard, so all he saw were mouth gestures. When he realized that she was actually praying and was not drunk, he blessed her and encouraged her to go in peace, assuring her that God would grant her request. And grant her request, God did. She conceived and gave birth to a son whom she named Samuel, who became a prophet of the Lord. In her gratitude, she recognized that Samuel was not just a personal blessing but also a fulfillment of God's faithfulness to her.

Hannah's gratitude is expressed in 1 Samuel 2, through a heartfelt song of praise known as the "Song of Hannah." In this prayer, she celebrated God's sovereignty, holiness, and the reversal of fortunes, how He lifts the humble and brings down the proud. She acknowledged that her experiences of barrenness and subsequent blessing were part of God's greater plan, revealing her deep understanding of God's character and faithfulness. Hannah's gratitude culminated in her fulfilling her vow by bringing Samuel to the temple after he was weaned and presenting him to Eli to serve in the house of the Lord. This act of dedication demonstrated her commitment to God and revealed her humility, as she recognized that her blessings were not only for her own enjoyment but were to be used in service to God. Overall, Hannah's story is an illustration of faith, perseverance, and gratitude. It emphasized the importance of acknowledging God's blessings and the call to use those blessings in service to others. Her journey from despair to joy served as a powerful testament to the transformative power of faith and gratitude in the life of a believer.

The Irresponsible & Entitled Son

The Prodigal Son in Luke 15:11-32 is a story of an entitled young man who demanded his inheritance from his father before his father has passed away. The son left home and squandered his wealth on reckless and debaucherous living. He eventually found himself in desperate circumstances after all of his money was gone and he had nothing to show for where it went. Asking for his share of the inheritance while his father was still alive, showed great disrespect and an entitlement to instant gratification. The young man disregarded cultural norms and familial respect. Inheritance is typically given after a parent's death, so his demand for his inheritance before the time reflected an expectation that he should receive what he felt "entitled" to, regardless of the implications. His request also showed a lack of consideration for his father's feelings. Instead of expressing gratitude for the care and support provided by his family, he focused solely on his own selfish and material desires, revealing a self-centered attitude. However, despite his egregious and entitled behavior, and after squandering all of his inheritance, he returned home and was met with an outpouring of love and forgiveness from his father, who celebrated his return. The older brother, however, displayed contempt, ingratitude and resentment, feeling entitled to more recognition for his loyalty while neglecting to appreciate the joy of his brother's redemption.

To show more gratitude in life, you can regularly reflect on and appreciate the positive aspects of daily experiences. Keeping a gratitude journal can help document and reinforce the constant blessings that you receive. Expressing appreciation verbally or through handwritten notes to others can also strengthen relationships. Engaging in acts of kindness, whether small or large, can also demonstrate gratitude. Being deliberate about acknowledging and celebrating the contributions of others fosters a culture of appreciation in both personal and professional settings. Let's be intentional about having an attitude of gratitude.

Lessons to Live By:

- When you are genuinely thankful for even the smallest things, God blesses you with more, and the blessings continue pouring in.

- Gratitude is not just a feeling or sentiment, but an active choice. It requires intentionality in your thoughts and actions, and a sincere appreciation for all that you have.

- Entitlement reflects a belief that one deserves certain privileges or benefits without necessarily earning them or working for them.

- Entitlement is a vice because it fosters self-centeredness, leading people to prioritize their own needs over everyone else's.

- When you approach life with humility, you are more inclined to appreciate the small joys and acts of kindness that might otherwise go unnoticed.

11

Joy & Anger

Joy uplifts the spirit and brings light and peace, while anger darkens perspective, consuming inner peace. Choosing joy over anger opens the heart to life's beauty, while anger blinds us to its blessings.

Joy and anger are two opposing emotions in our lives. Joy is a deep and lasting sense of contentment rooted in our relationship with God. It flourishes through faith, hope, and trust in His promises, transcending the chaos of our circumstances. True joy emanates from recognizing the deep and pure love of our Creator, reminding us that our worth and happiness do not hinge on external situations but on the unchanging nature of God. As believers, we are invited to cultivate joy even in the midst of life's challenges. As believers, we have access to a joy that is not dependent on the ups and downs of life, but on the unchanging character of our Lord. It can be easy to focus on all of the negatives in our lives and allow them to steal our joy, but as believers, we are able to look beyond our circumstances and turn to the peace and contentment that is already within us. Regardless of what is happening in the world around us, we can turn within and cultivate the joy that comes from God. When you stay in God's presence, you experience the fullness of what joy truly is, as it is written in Psalm 16:11, *"...in thy presence is fullness of joy."* Joy is a deep and lasting sense of contentment because it is grounded in something more permanent than temporary pleasures or circumstances. When I say that joy is "lasting," I mean that it endures over time and remains resolute even when the circumstances of life change.

Joy v/s Happiness

Joy is not the same as happiness. It is a deep-rooted state of gladness and contentment that comes from something greater than life or external situations. Joy is often associated with the presence of the Holy Spirit and is a fruit of the Spirit, as noted in Galatians 5:22-23. Spiritual joy is tied to faith, hope, and trust in God's promises, and it is often revealed even in the midst of trials, as illustrated in James 1:2-3: *My brethren, count it all joy when ye fall into divers temptations, knowing this, that the trying of your faith worketh patience.* The joy described in that scripture is grounded in the assurance of God's love, salvation, and eternal promises, offering us a sense of fulfillment and peace.

From a worldly perspective, joy is generally understood as a feeling of great pleasure, delight, or happiness often triggered by external circumstances or events, personal achievements, or happy relationships. More often than not, worldly joy is temporary and linked to external factors that can change. This kind of joy is more about emotional satisfaction and the fulfillment of desires, making it susceptible to life's vicissitudes. One thing that makes joy stand so far apart from happiness is that it can coexist with trials, sorrow, or pain, because it is based on a spiritual connection rather than external conditions. Happiness is framed around situations that are going well, but joy can be present when things are not going well. Happiness is usually dependent on favorable outcomes and positive external circumstances. It is an emotional response to external events, but joy is not emotional, and it is not a response. It is something internal that resides on the inside of one's heart and soul, independent of external factors. Joy is a virtue because it embodies a moral quality that reflects a state of inner well-being, resilience, and alignment with spiritual truth. As a virtue, joy represents more than a feeling, but rather a character trait cultivated through intentional practice, even in the face of adversity. By maintaining joy, we demonstrate trust in God's sovereignty and goodness, showing spiritual maturity and a steadfast spirit even in difficult times.

Anger

Anger is an intense emotional response to actual or perceived wrongs, injustices, misunderstandings, or frustrations. It can be demonstrated through verbal expressions such as shouting or criticizing, physical actions such as slamming or punching objects or aggressive or violent behavior such as physical abuse or the use of objects to harm someone or something. Uncontrollable anger is dangerous because it clouds judgment and often leads to impulsive or harmful actions that damage relationships, reputations, and can sometimes change the entire course of one's life.

Healthy anger is a constructive response that acknowledges feelings of frustration or injustice while remaining controlled and intentional. Healthy anger serves a positive purpose, like setting boundaries, addressing wrongs, or motivating change. This kind of anger is expressed calmly and assertively. It allows for effective and mature communication, rational resolutions, and personal growth without causing harm to oneself or others. Unhealthy anger, on the other hand, is reactive, excessive, or uncontrollable, fueled by resentment, and leading to aggression, hostility, or passive-aggressive behaviors. This type of anger damages relationships, increases stress levels, and creates a cycle of negativity, because it lacks productive outlets and often escalates conflict.

Godly Anger

Godly anger is rooted in righteousness and is motivated by a desire for justice, holiness, and the protection of what is good. Godly anger arises when God's will, love, or commands are violated. An example of this can be found in Matthew 21:12-13 when Jesus expressed anger in the temple over the corruption and exploitation that was going on there.

And Jesus went into the temple of God, and cast out all them that sold and bought in the temple, and overthrew the tables of the moneychangers, and the seats of them that sold doves. And said unto them, It is written, My house shall be called the house of prayer; but ye have made it a den of thieves.

Godly anger remains controlled and purposeful, seeking to correct wrongs and leads to reconciliation, repentance, or positive change. It is guided by love and seeks to align with God's will.

Worldly Anger

Worldly anger on the other hand, is driven by self-interest, pride, or personal offense and is typically focused on satisfying one's own desires or reacting impulsively to unmet expectations. This kind of anger is usually fueled by ego, vengeance, or selfish motives, which often leads to bitterness, hostility, or revenge. This anger is destructive, lacks control, and rarely produces any good outcomes, because it prioritizes self and personal feelings over spiritual principles. It can become a destructive and harmful emotion when it is uncontrolled, excessive, or misdirected. As a vice, it undermines virtues such as patience, love, and self-control, leading to negative outcomes like broken relationships, poor decision-making, and regretful actions.

When anger becomes habitual or is expressed aggressively, it births bitterness, hostility, and resentment, causing harm to others and oneself. It often leads to conflict rather than resolution, as it focuses more on reacting to a wrong than on correcting it constructively. Uncontrolled and worldly anger cloud judgment, fuel revenge, and prevent individuals from exhibiting compassion or forgiveness, making them a barrier to spiritual growth, moral character, and personal peace. Their potential to escalate into more severe destructive behaviors, such as violence or abuse, further solidifies their classifications as vices.

Cain's Anger

The story of Cain and Abel shows us how unchecked anger can escalate into tragic and irreversible consequences. Cain and Abel were brothers and were the sons of Adam and Eve, our first parents.

Both brothers brought offerings to God as they were instructed to do. Abel offered a firstborn lamb from his flock, and Cain offered fruits from his crops. God accepted Abel's offering but rejected Cain's offering likely because Abel's was presented in faith, love and with a sincere heart, while Cain's lacked the same devotion (Genesis 4:4-5). Cain became angry and resentful toward his brother, feeling rejected and humiliated. However, instead of correcting his attitude, checking his heart, and focusing on rectifying the problem, he allowed his anger to fester, which led him to commit the horrendous act of murdering his brother. Cain likely took his frustrations out on Abel because Abel's offering symbolized what Cain's lacked, which was faith, righteousness, and favor with God. Abel, by doing nothing wrong, inadvertently became a reminder of Cain's own shortcomings and failure to please God. Consumed by jealousy and resentment, Cain allowed his anger to shift from God to Abel, seeing him as the cause for his frustration. Instead of addressing his own faults or seeking God's guidance, Cain's uncontrolled anger drove him to eliminate what he thought was the source of his envy, leading to Abel's murder.

The story of Cain and Abel demonstrates the devastating potential of unchecked anger. Initially, Cain's anger was rooted in rejection and envy over God favoring Abel's offering. Instead of managing his emotions or seeking reconciliation with God, Cain nurtured resentment and allowed it to grow into hatred and violence. God even warned Cain that sin was crouching at his door, urging him to master his anger: *If thou doest well, shalt thou not be accepted? and if thou doest not well, sin lieth at the door* (Genesis 4:7). But Cain ignored this warning, and his unchecked anger led to the first murder, demonstrating how anger, when left to fester, can transform into destructive actions with irreversible consequences. This murder of Abel marked the first act of human violence following Adam and Eve's disobedience, showcasing how sin quickly escalated from disobedience in the Garden of Eden to premeditated

> *"Choosing to nurture joy while taming anger is not merely about achieving personal peace; it is a spiritual pursuit that honors God."*

murder. This tragic event illustrated the depth of humanity's fallen nature, with anger, jealousy, and sin leading to devastating consequences.

Cain's Consequences

As a result of shedding Abel's innocent blood, God declared that Cain would be cursed from the ground, meaning that the soil would no longer yield crops for him, making his work unfruitful (Genesis 4:11-12). Additionally, Cain was condemned to be a restless wanderer on the earth, a vagabond. After hearing his punishment, Cain expressed fear of being killed by others, so God marked him with a protective sign, ensuring that anyone who killed him would suffer vengeance sevenfold (Genesis 4:15). These consequences given to Cain for murder, emphasized the gravity of his sin and the profound effects of shedding innocent blood.

Evaluating our anger is crucial because it helps us identify the true source of the anger, whether it stems from rejection, hurt, fear, pride, unmet expectations, or deeper unresolved issues. Understanding where anger is coming from allows us to address the root cause rather than reacting impulsively, which often leads to destructive consequences. Self-awareness in moments of anger can help prevent it from escalating into harmful actions or words, as seen in Cain's story. I have identified some strategies for attempting to put anger in check if applicable to you:

1. **Pause and reflect**: Take a moment to calm down and understand why you are feeling angry. Does the level of the situation match your level of anger?

2. **Pray or meditate**: Seek spiritual guidance or inner peace to gain clarity and wisdom in handling your emotions.

3. **Communicate openly**: Express your feelings calmly and assertively, aiming for constructive dialogue rather than conflict.

4. **Practice empathy**: Consider the other person's perspective, which can often reduce anger and increase understanding.

5. **Seek forgiveness**: If anger arises from feeling wronged, actively work toward forgiveness, which can diffuse bitterness.

6. **Develop self-control**: Cultivate patience, self-discipline, and restraint, using spiritual teachings or practical techniques like deep breathing.

By regularly evaluating and managing our anger, we align more closely with God's will, promote inner peace, and nurture healthier relationships. Below are several scriptures from the King James Version that address anger and managing it:

- **Proverbs 16:32:**
  He that is slow to anger is better than the mighty; and he that ruleth his spirit than he that taketh a city.

- **Proverbs 25:28:**
  He that hath no rule over his own spirit is like a city that is broken down, and without walls.

- **Ecclesiastes 7:9:**
  Be not hasty in thy spirit to be angry: for anger resteth in the bosom of fools.

- **Ephesians 4:26:**
  Be ye angry, and sin not: let not the sun go down upon your wrath.

- **James 1:19-20:**
  Wherefore, my beloved brethren, let every man be swift to hear, slow to speak, slow to wrath: For the wrath of man worketh not the righteousness of God.

- ❧ **Proverbs 14:29:**
  He that is slow to wrath is of great understanding: but he that is hasty of spirit exalteth folly.

- ❧ **Proverbs 15:1:**
  A soft answer turneth away wrath: but grievous words stir up anger.

- ❧ **Psalm 37:8:**
  Cease from anger and forsake wrath: fret not thyself in any wise to do evil.

- ❧ **Colossians 3:8:**
  But now ye also put off all these; anger, wrath, malice, blasphemy, filthy communication out of your mouth.

- ❧ **Proverbs 29:11:**
  A fool uttereth all his mind: but a wise man keepeth it in till afterwards.

These verses offer both warnings against uncontrolled anger and guidance on how to manage it righteously. If you are someone who has an anger problem, take heed to the Word of God and let those words resonate deeply within you. Practice self-control and pray for strength in this area to eradicate your anger.

The Ethiopian Eunuch who Found Great Joy

In Acts 8:27, there was an Ethiopian eunuch who was a high-ranking official under Candace, the Queen of Ethiopia. He had come to Jerusalem to worship and was returning back home from his journey. He was likely a God-fearing Gentile who revered the God of Israel and had traveled to Jerusalem for religious purposes when Philip encountered him in Acts 8:30-31. He was reading the book of Isaiah, but did not quite understanding the meaning or significance of what he was reading until Phillip explained to him that those verses were about Jesus: *And Philip ran thither to him, and heard him read the prophet Esaias (Isaiah) and said, Understandest thou what thou readest? And he said, How can I, except some man should guide me? And he desired Philip that he would come up and sit with him.*

After understanding the message that Philip had explained to him, he was moved and asked to be baptized when they came upon water. After his baptism, he left rejoicing, having found enlightenment, salvation, a new faith in Christ, and great joy. Realizing that the prophecy pointed to Jesus as the promised Messiah who came to save all people, including Gentiles such as himself, he experienced a spiritual awakening, and a desire for redemption. The joy that emerged in him is highlighted in Acts 8:39, where it states that after his baptism, he *"went on his way rejoicing."* This reaction suggests that the act of baptism, coupled with his newfound understanding of Jesus as the Messiah, brought him profound spiritual joy. The realization of salvation, acceptance by God, and being part of the Christian faith likely filled him with inner peace, fulfillment, and enlightenment as he continued his journey.

Joy and anger, though opposite in nature, have significant power over our lives, influencing our thoughts, actions, and outcomes. Joy, when cultivated intentionally, brings peace, contentment, and fulfillment, aligning us with God's purpose and promoting lasting peace even in challenging times. It is a virtue that uplifts, strengthens relationships, and fosters spiritual growth. Conversely, anger, when left unchecked, becomes a destructive vice that distorts judgment, damages relationships, and can lead to devastating consequences. However, when managed properly, anger can serve as a catalyst for positive change, prompting us to address wrongs and seek justice in righteous ways. Ultimately, choosing to nurture joy while taming anger is not merely about achieving personal peace; it is a spiritual pursuit that honors God, blesses others, and leads to a more balanced, meaningful life. As we journey through life's highs and lows, may we seek to foster the virtue of joy and harness the potential of anger for constructive purposes, aligning both emotions with Divine wisdom.

- The source of true joy is not found in circumstances or situations happening around us, but in our relationship with our Creator through Jesus Christ.

- When you stay in God's presence, you experience the fullness of what joy truly is.

- Happiness is usually dependent on favorable outcomes and positive circumstances. It is an emotional response to external events.

- Healthy anger serves a positive purpose, like setting boundaries, addressing wrongs, or motivating change.

- Godly anger is rooted in righteousness and is motivated by a desire for justice, holiness, and the protection of what is good.

12

Patience & Impulsivity

Patience waits with purpose, allowing growth and wisdom to unfold, while impulsivity rushes ahead, often leading to regret. Embracing patience cultivates resilience, while impulsivity scatters intentions, robbing us of deeper, lasting rewards.

Patience is often regarded as the ability to endure discomfort or delay without frustration. It serves as a cornerstone of emotional intelligence and maturity. Patience is not passively waiting, but an active state of perseverance and composure, allowing us to navigate the complexities of life with grace. The benefits of patience are many. For one, it fosters resilience and enables us to withstand challenges and setbacks with a balanced perspective. In our fast-paced world, where instant gratification has become the norm, exercising patience can lead to deeper understanding and appreciation of our experiences. The virtue of patience embodies the qualities of self-control, calmness and wisdom. It also reflects am understanding that not everything unfolds according to our personal timelines, but in God's timing, which is almost always contradictory to our time. As we explore the dynamic interplay between patience and impulsivity, we are reminded that cultivating patience not only enriches our lives but also serves as a testament to our character and spiritual maturity.

Impulsivity

In contrast, impulsivity is characterized by the tendency to act on whims or immediate desires without fully considering the consequences of your actions. This lack of forethought can manifest in effusive behaviors, ranging from minor decisions to significant life choices. Impulsivity often arises from emotional reactions, mental instability or a desire for instant gratification, leading one to prioritize short-term satisfaction over long-term well-being. Impulsivity is considered a vice because it subverts self-control and rational decision-making. When we act impulsively, we may disregard important factors such as the impact on others or the long-term effects of our choices. This tendency can perpetuate patterns of behavior that are inconsistent with our values or goals, ultimately leading to regret and self-destructive outcomes. The destructive nature of impulsivity can manifest in several ways. Financially, impulsive spending can lead to debt and financial instability. Impulsive reactions during conflicts can damage relationships and create rifts that are difficult to repair. In a broader sense, impulsivity can also lead to risky behaviors, such as substance abuse, reckless driving, or unsafe sexual practices, putting you in precarious situations that can have lasting consequences. Some people are in prison today with no chance of ever integrating with outside society for impulsive decisions they made in a moment of impulsivity. That moment changed the entire course of their lives. Ultimately, impulsivity can create a cycle of negative situations when the immediate thrill or relief experienced from impulsive actions is often followed by feelings of guilt, shame, or anxiety. By failing to pause and reflect, we may find ourselves trapped in a pattern that continues in dissatisfaction and turmoil, highlighting the importance of cultivating patience as a counterbalance to impulsivity.

The Consequences of Impulsivity

The Bible teaches the importance of patience, both through positive examples like Hannah and Elizabeth and negative examples of impatience like Abraham and Saul. Abraham is a prime example of what can happen when we lack patience and take matters into our own hands. God promised him and Sarah a child, but as the years passed with no baby in sight and Sarah remaining barren, Abraham became anxious and impatient. Through the persuading of his wife, He agreed to conceive a child with her maid, Hagar. This decision led to chaos and serious problems in Abraham's bloodline for years to come. The results of Abraham's impatience still wreak havoc today and has been a devastating historical reality for the descendants of both Ismael and Isaac.

Hannah and Elizabeth's Patience

In contrast, Hannah and Elizabeth are examples of the fruit of patience. They were unable to have children for years, but instead of becoming anxious or giving up hope, they patiently prayed and waited for God's timing. Their patience was rewarded when they finally gave birth to God-fearing, anointed sons: Samuel, who would become a great prophet in Israel and John, who would be the forerunner for Christ, the Savior. As Christians, we are called to be patient and trust in God's timing. We may not always understand why things seem to take so long, but we can trust that God has a plan and that He is in control.

Patience can be a struggle for many, especially in a world that values instant gratification and fast-paced results. In today's world, we become impatient over the smallest things. It is easy to become frustrated and discouraged when things don't happen as quickly or easily as we want them to, but when we wait on the Lord, we can find renewed strength, patience, and peace. Our focus shifts from our own desires for immediate results to the power and provision of God. Waiting on the Lord means being still and allowing His timing to work in our lives. It means trusting that He has a plan and understanding that His timing is always perfect, even if it comes at the 11th hour.

The Priceless Gift of Patience

In the Gospel of Luke, there is a righteous and devout man named Simeon who is introduced. The text does not offer much about him as it pertains to his background or personal life. However, his brief appearance in scripture serves to emphasize his virtues of faith, patience, and Divine promises. He is described as a man of God who was very attuned to the ear of God. The Holy Spirit had revealed to him that he would not die before seeing the "Lord's Messiah." This direct communication revealed his close relationship with God and his role as a faithful servant. Simeon patiently waited for the day when he could behold with his own eyes, the world's Savior. This specific mention of being "moved by the Spirit" demonstrated that Simeon was responsive to Divine guidance. The timing of his arrival at the temple coinciding with Mary and Joseph's presentation of Jesus illustrated the fulfillment of the promise he had received. His experience with the infant Jesus was profound, as he recognized Him as the fulfillment of God's promise. After seeing Jesus, Simeon offered a blessing, indicating that he understood the child's mission in God's plan for salvation. Simeon's story demonstrates how God honors those who remain faithful and patient in their hope for His promises. Luke 2:25-30:

*And, behold, there was a man in Jerusalem, whose name was Simeon; and the same man was just and devout, waiting for the consolation of Israel: and the Holy Ghost was upon him. And it was revealed unto him by the Holy Ghost, that he should not see death, before he had seen the Lord's Christ. And he came **by the Spirit** into the temple: and when the parents brought in the child Jesus, to do for him after the custom of the law. Then took he him up in his arms, and blessed God, and said, Lord, now lettest thou thy servant depart in peace, according to thy word. For mine eyes have seen thy salvation.*

Simeon likely experienced profound feelings of joy, fulfillment, and peace upon finally seeing the Messiah after a long period of waiting. His patience and faith would have cultivated a deep sense of anticipation, so the moment when he held Jesus in his arms would have been both exhilarating and emotionally overwhelming. In my opinion, he

> *"Patience is not passively waiting, but an active state of perseverance and composure, allowing us to navigate the complexities of life with grace."*

would have felt a sense of vindication, knowing that the promise he received from the Holy Spirit had finally come to fruition. This fulfillment reaffirmed his faith and devotion throughout the years and solidified his belief in God's faithfulness. In his prayer of thanksgiving, Simeon expressed his contentment confirming that he was ready to transition in peace, having seen the salvation that God had sent. This moment represented not only personal joy, but also the hope and redemption for Israel and humanity as a whole. Overall, Simeon's experience reflected a culmination of longing, faith, and the deep satisfaction that came from witnessing the fulfillment of God's promises.

Practicing patience often pays off. It allows us to navigate challenges and setbacks with calmness and leads to better decision-making. By taking the time to reflect rather than reacting impulsively, we can often achieve favorable outcomes. In relationships, patience fosters understanding and empathy and enhances communication and trust. In personal or professional goals, those who remain patient may find that their hard work and perseverance eventually lead to successful outcomes, as they are more likely to stick with their efforts through difficult times. The waiting period can often lead to personal growth, deeper faith, and ultimately, the fulfillment of desires in ways that may be more meaningful than immediate gratification. While the process of waiting can be challenging, the rewards of patience often manifest in positive and transformative ways.

Lessons to Live By:

- Patience reflects a deep understanding that not everything unfolds according to our personal timelines, but in God's timing,

- Patience is a virtue because it embodies the qualities of self-control, wisdom, and humility.

- Impulsivity is characterized by the tendency to act on whims or immediate desires without fully considering the consequences of your actions.
- Some people are in prison right now with no chance of parole for impulsive decisions they made in a moment.

- The waiting period can often lead to personal growth, deeper faith, and ultimately, the fulfillment of desires in ways that may be more meaningful than immediate gratification.

13

Humility & Pride

Humility grounds us in truth and opens the heart to wisdom and growth, while pride elevates the self and closes off understanding. Choosing humility fosters connection and grace, while pride isolates, leading to a fall.

To be humble is to have a modest opinion of yourself, recognizing your limitations and valuing others for their uniqueness and innate gifts. Humility is a virtue that God honors because it shows that one realizes that they can do nothing alone but that all they have comes from God through others. Humility develops from a willingness to grow beyond one's ego. Cultivating a mindset of learning rather than competing with others helps to maintain humility. It is also important to note that a person can be both humble and confident at the same time. Confidence emerges from a strong sense of self-worth and belief in one's self-efficacy while humility embraces a continuous mindset to learn and help others. Together, these traits allow you to acknowledge your strengths without arrogance and remain open to learning and to receiving constructive criticism. This balance fosters emotional intelligence, maturity, healthy relationships and promotes personal growth. People who are humble yet confident inspire trust and respect in others. Oftentimes, we see individuals who are extremely wealthy or influential but lack humility. They are not grounded and are often dismissive towards those who are not on their level from a financial or prominent standpoint.

However, a person can be highly successful or wealthy and still be humble. This balance is achieved by maintaining a grounded perspective, while recognizing that their success does not diminish the value of others. Humble people often prioritize gratitude, share their wealth and success with others, and remain accessible despite their status. They focus on continuous personal growth and seek to uplift those around them rather than seeking validation and attention because of their achievements. Humility reduces arrogance and entitlement and leads to a more balanced and respectful approach to life. Humility also makes room for receiving wisdom and insight, leading to personal and spiritual development. Dependence on God is the foundation of humility and promotes an open mindset leading to stronger relationships. One who practices the Law of Humility is always open to being taught; they are receptive to correction and are open to learning from others while acknowledging that they do not have all the answers. One who practices humility values the contributions and perspectives of others, which lays a foundation for mutual respect and trust. This humble mindset creates a supportive and collaborative environment, and strengthens connections with family, friends, and colleagues.

False Humility

The difference between genuine humility and false humility lies in the intention and authenticity behind the expressions of modesty. Humility is a genuine recognition of one's limitations and an appreciation for the value of others. Those who are humble have an accurate self-assessment and do not seek validation from anybody; instead, they confidently acknowledge their strengths and work on their weaknesses while remaining open to learning from others. In contrast, false humility involves a deceptive display of modesty, often to gain approval or manipulate perceptions. Individuals exhibiting false humility may downplay their achievements or abilities, not out of genuine modesty but rather to elicit praise or recognition. This act is insincere and may mask underlying arrogance, as the focus remains on self rather than on a true appreciation for others. In essence, true humility stems from authenticity and self-awareness, while false humility is rooted in a desire for recognition and approval.

The Humble Prayer of Jabez

The story of Jabez and his humility is found in 1 Chronicles 4:9-10, where Jabez, whose name means "sorrow" or "pain" in Hebrew asks God to bless him, enlarge his territory, be with him, and keep him from harm. He was given his name by his mother because of the pain she endured while giving birth to him. His name signified a life destined for hardship or sorrow for him. In biblical times, names carried significant meanings and were believed to influence a person's character or destiny. Jabez's name implied a life filled with suffering, but instead of accepting this fate, he displayed humility and faith by turning to God in prayer. He acknowledged his limitations and sought Divine intervention to change the trajectory of his life. His humble request reflected his desire for God's favor, blessings and guidance. This showed a recognition of his dependence on God rather than on himself. By asking God to enlarge his territory, he sought opportunities for growth and success beyond what his name suggested. His prayer displayed the power of humility and faith, and demonstrated how to turn to God, which can lead to transformation and a life defined by Divine purpose rather than human limitations.

Turning to God with sincerity demonstrates humility because it involves acknowledging your limitations, weaknesses, and your need for Divine assistance, something that a human cannot give. This reflects a recognition that we as humans cannot rely solely on our own strength or understanding but we need God's guidance and support in every area of our lives. Sincere prayer and supplication are found in a heart that is willing to submit to God's will, trust in His plans, and seek His wisdom. Humility moves the heart of God and scripture often emphasizes God's favor toward the humble. When we approach God with a humble spirit, it creates an atmosphere where we can receive His grace and blessings. Humble hearts are open to transformation and growth and allows God to work in the life of the humble more effectively.

Pride

In contrast, unhealthy pride is marked by an inflated sense of self-importance and superiority. It often leads to arrogance, entitlement, and a lack of empathy for others. Individuals who are lifted in pride often prioritize their successes and achievements over others, which results in a competitive mindset that can alienate and diminish relationships. Pride includes a sense of superiority and self-worth derived from one's perceived achievements, skills, or possessions. It can mask itself as confidence and self-assurance but when excessive, it leads to arrogance or an inflated sense of self-importance. This kind of pride often involves comparing oneself favorably to others and making others look significantly diminutive in comparison.

The difference between pride and healthy self-confidence lies in focus, motivation, and impact on relationships. Unhealthy pride is self-centered and is rooted in an inflated sense of one's abilities or status. It seeks recognition and places oneself above others. However, a healthy self-confidence is grounded in an accurate understanding and awareness of one's abilities and worth. It is self-assured but balanced by humility and acknowledges strengths while remaining open to learning and improvement. Unlike unhealthy pride, self-confidence is not about demonstrating superiority but about embracing God-given gifts that contribute positively to others, the world, and one's personal growth. A healthy self-confidence fosters constructive relationships, teamwork, and a willingness to listen and adapt. In essence, unhealthy pride isolates and elevates oneself, while healthy self-confidence empowers and encourages both personal and collective success. Pride is a vice because it often leads to arrogance, entitlement, and a diminished capacity for empathy. Excessive pride causes you to overestimate your worth and become oblivious to the contributions and talents of others around you, which strains relationships and breeds resentment. This inflated self-perception can hinder personal growth and create barriers to learning, which can ultimately result a lack of genuine connection.

Healthy Pride

Healthy pride can be referred to as self-respect or dignity which are positive forms of pride. This type of pride comes from a sense of satisfaction in one's achievements, integrity, and moral principles. It's a balanced pride that promotes confidence without arrogance and encourages personal growth. For example, one can have pride in knowing that their children do well in school. One can have pride in themselves for earning a college degree. One can take great pride in knowing they have a capable and competent team of supporters around them. While a healthy level of pride can motivate individuals to pursue their goals and celebrate their successes, excessive pride can result in entitlement and a resistance to feedback, ultimately hindering personal growth and relationships.

Characteristics of Unhealthy Pride:

- **Arrogance**: A belief in one's superiority over others, often leading to dismissive behavior

- **Entitlement**: A sense that one deserves special treatment or recognition without necessarily earning it

- **Lack of Empathy**: Difficulty in understanding or valuing the feelings and perspectives of others

- **Inflexibility**: Resistance to feedback or criticism, often stemming from an inflated self-image

- **Comparison**: Frequently measuring oneself favorably against others to reinforce a sense of superiority

- **Self-Centeredness**: A focus on personal achievements and recognition rather than collective success or teamwork

- **Defensiveness**: Reacting negatively when challenged or confronted, often perceiving feedback as a threat to self-worth

- **Difficulty in Acknowledging Mistakes**: Struggling to accept fault or apologize, as this may conflict with a proud self-image

Pride can lead to a great downfall when one continuously feeds their inflated sense of self-importance. This arrogance prevents them from seeking help or advice and ultimately leads to poor decision-making. Pride often results in a lack of empathy, which creates strained relationships and alienation from others. The Bible warns against pride and emphasizes that it can lead to a downfall and separation from God. Proverbs 16:18 states that, *"Pride goes before destruction,"* indicating that arrogance often precedes a big or humiliating failure. The Bible also teaches that humility is favored by God, as seen in James 4:6, which says, *"God opposes the proud but gives grace to the humble."* Furthermore, it is written in Proverbs 11:2 that, *"When pride comes, then comes shame"* highlighting the negative consequences of a proud heart. Overall, the scriptures encourage believers to embrace humility and rely on God rather than self-sufficiency or arrogance.

King Nebuchadnezzar's Great Pride

An example of someone who was lifted up in pride to their own detriment is King Nebuchadnezzar of Babylon, as depicted in the Book of Daniel in the Bible. Nebuchadnezzar's pride was evident when he constructed a massive golden statue and commanded everyone to bow down and worship it. This act alone displayed his arrogance and belief in his own power and strength, as he sought to establish himself as a god. His pride culminated in a moment of hubris in Daniel 4:30, when he boasted about all of his accomplishments, saying, *"Is not this the great Babylon **I** have built as the royal residence, by **my** mighty power and for the glory of **my** majesty?"* This statement clearly revealed his inflated ego and disregard for God's sovereignty. Ultimately, God severely humbled him by removing his sanity causing him to live in the wilderness like a wild animal for seven years. He was driven away from the people, ate grass like cattle, and his body was drenched with the "dew of heaven." His hair grew long like eagles' feathers, and his nails became like bird claws.

This period of seven years symbolized Nebuchadnezzar's complete judgment until he recognized and acknowledged God's sovereignty. After acknowledging God as the true ruler, his sanity was restored, and he was returned to his kingdom. This story highlighted the consequences of pride and serves as a powerful lesson on the importance of humility before God. After King Nebuchadnezzar's restoration back to his right mind, he praised the God of the universe and acknowledged that true power and sovereignty belonged to Him and Him alone.

"I" "Me" and "Mine"

This above story also underscored how the constant use of the words "I" and "my" and "mine" are often indicative of a self-centered person who may have a pride issue. Frequent and constant references to self often reflect an inflated sense of self-importance and an unhealthy focus on one's personal achievements with no mention of the help of others. When individuals constantly emphasize "I" in their conversations, it may suggest that they prioritize their own experiences and successes over others. This often manifests itself in conversations where a person dominates discussions while seeking validation or recognition without considering the contributions or feelings of others. While self-reference is not necessarily problematic, an excessive focus on "I" can be a sign of pride and may hinder meaningful interactions.

In a world that often equates success with titles, position, money and status, the journey towards humility is both essential and transformative. Embracing humility allows us to recognize our limitations and appreciate the unique gifts of others. This creates a foundation for mutual respect and bonding. As illustrated by Jabez' earnest prayer and

> *"Pride can lead to a great downfall when one continuously feeds their inflated sense of self-importance."*

the humbling experience of King Nebuchadnezzar, true strength lies not in boasting or in self-exaltation, but in dependence on God. By fostering humility, we not only invite God's grace and blessings into our lives, but we also cultivate deeper, more meaningful relationships. In contrast to pride, which isolates and alienates, humility bonds people together, promotes emotional intelligence, and enhances our capacity for growth. Therefore, let us strive to cultivate a humble heart and remain open to learning and growing, as we seek to honor God and uplift those around us. In doing so, we align ourselves with a purpose that transcends personal achievement, creating a life rich in fulfillment and genuine connection.

Lessons to Live By:

- A person can be both humble and confident at the same time. Confidence emerges from a strong sense of self-worth and belief in one's self-efficacy

- A person can be highly successful or wealthy and still be humble. This balance is achieved by maintaining a grounded perspective while recognizing that their success does not diminish the value of others.

- False humility involves a deceptive display of modesty, often to gain approval or manipulate perceptions.

- Unhealthy pride is marked by an inflated sense of self-importance and superiority. It often leads to arrogance, entitlement, and a lack of empathy for others.

- The difference between pride and healthy self-confidence lies in focus, motivation, and impact on relationships.

14

Generosity & Greed

Generosity opens the heart to give freely which creates abundance and joy, while greed clutches tightly and creates emptiness and isolation. Choosing generosity enriches the soul, while greed consumes and leaves a void nothing can fill.

To be generous means to willingly give of your time, resources, kindness, or service without expecting anything in return. Generosity involves a spirit of giving, where one seeks to share rather than acquire. It is often characterized by empathy, compassion, and a desire to uplift others, even at a personal sacrifice. Generosity reflects an open heart, driven by love and a genuine desire to help people. Generosity is a virtue because it displays selflessness, compassion, and a commitment to the well-being of others. It embodies the moral excellence of giving freely without expecting anything in return and reveals kindness, empathy, and an open-hearted spirit. It also cultivates abundance, fosters gratitude and a deeper connection with others. Generosity promotes harmony and enriches both the giver and the receiver. As a virtue, it aligns with ethical and spiritual principles that prioritize serving others, helping others and supporting others. The Bible embraces generosity as a virtue that reflects God's love and brings blessings. Proverbs 11:25 states, *"The liberal soul shall be made fat: and he that watereth shall be watered also himself"* highlighting how giving benefits both the giver and the receiver. In 2 Corinthians 9:6-7, Paul emphasizes the spirit behind giving: *"He which soweth sparingly shall reap also sparingly; and he which soweth bountifully shall reap also bountifully. Every man according as he purposeth in his heart, so let him give; not grudgingly, or of necessity: for God loveth a cheerful giver."* This verse clearly highlights the spirit of the giver. Releasing what you have with a cheerful heart brings blessings, but when a person gives reluctantly or with a begrudging heart, the act loses much of its spiritual value. While the material benefit of the gift may still help others, the giver misses out on the deeper blessings that come from a heart aligned with God's principles. The attitude behind the gift matters as much as the gift itself. A reluctant or begrudging heart reflects a lack of trust in God's provision and an absence of joy in serving others. Instead of fostering spiritual growth, such giving can lead to resentment or a sense of obligation, robbing the giver of the joy and peace that come from generosity. Ultimately, true blessings flow when giving is motivated by love, faith, and a genuine desire to bless others, rather than by duty or reluctance.

Generosity is seen as an act of faith, trusting that God will provide and multiply resources to meet your needs and the needs of others. In Luke 6:38, Jesus also tells us that we should, *"Give, and it shall be given unto you"* teaches that generous giving invites God's blessings. The Bible portrays generosity as a natural expression of love and compassion, rooted in a desire to serve and honor God by helping others. Giving and receiving are interconnected. As one hand gives, it makes room for the other to receive, allowing blessings to flow freely. The invisible blessing is the abundance that arises when a person maintains a balance of giving with an open heart and receiving with gratitude. The enhances both material and spiritual prosperity. Generosity reflects a life of abundance, stimulated by faith in God's provision and the joy of being a conduit for His blessings.

Joseph of Arimathea

Joseph of Arimathea was a wealthy and respected member of the Jewish council who showed remarkable generosity after Jesus was crucified. Despite the potential risks to his status and safety, Joseph boldly approached Pilate (who was the Roman governor at the time), to request Jesus' body. Joseph then provided his own new tomb, which was a costly and sacred possession, to ensure Jesus received an honorable burial. This act of generosity of providing Jesus' tomb fulfilled prophecy written hundreds of years earlier by the Prophet Isaiah in Isaiah 53:9, which stated, *"And he made his grave with the wicked, and with the rich in his death; because he had done no violence, neither was any deceit in his mouth."* Despite Jesus' crucifixion alongside criminals and His burial in a wealthy man's tomb fulfilled that prophecy. Isaiah's prophecy predicted that the "Suffering Servant", though despised and rejected, would be honored in death. Joseph's generous act not only provided Jesus with a dignified burial, but also confirmed God's Divine plan, aligning with scripture and validating Jesus as the prophesied Messiah.

Joseph's act of providing his brand new tomb for Jesus was considered profoundly generous because of the personal sacrifice and significance of the offering. In Jewish culture, a tomb was a family heirloom meant for one's own burial, representing both honor and legacy. It was costly to carve out and prepare which made it a precious and personal possession. By giving up this tomb, Joseph not only surrendered something of great monetary value but also relinquished his own burial place. Moreover, associating himself with Jesus, who had been publicly executed, risked Joseph's social standing and safety. His willingness to honor Jesus in this profound way, despite the potential repercussions, exemplified a level of generosity marked by selflessness, courage, and a deep reverence for Christ.

Greed

Greed is an excessive desire to acquire or possess more than you need, particularly regarding material possessions, wealth or power. It is characterized by selfishness, insatiable cravings, and a disregard for the well-being of others. Greed often leads to unethical behavior, hoarding, and exploitation, as individuals prioritize personal gain over moral principles or social responsibility. People often want more due to a combination of psychological, emotional, and societal factors. Psychologically, the pursuit of more can be driven by a natural desire for security, status, or a sense of achievement. Oftentimes this is rooted in one's upbringing where things were scarce, and they did not have much, so they make up for it by overcompensating for what they did not have growing up.

Emotionally, acquiring more is sometimes a coping mechanism for deeper insecurities, loneliness, or the need for validation. Sometimes people have an unhealthy habit of shopping excessively to mask their depression, heartbreak, or some other emotional turmoil that they may be going through. From a social standpoint, society often equates expensive material possessions or success to personal worth, creating constant pressure to accumulate more. In this case, people want material things such as houses, cars, jewelry or expensive clothes as status symbols so others can look at them and perceive that they are a successful and important person. Regardless of why, this perpetual drive for more is fueled by comparison, competition, and the belief that happiness or fulfillment can be achieved through external possessions or accomplishments. But greed never satisfies the desire for more. It creates a cycle of insatiable craving, where each time you get more, the desire for something bigger or better emerges again. This is because greed is rooted in discontent, so no amount of material possessions can fill the underlying emptiness it seeks to mask. Instead of fulfillment, greed often leads to greater dissatisfaction because the focus remains on what you don't have rather than on what you already have.

Greed is a vice, especially in the context of widespread poverty, because it exacerbates inequality and struggle. When those with wealth or power prioritize accumulation over compassion or helping those in need, it often results in the hoarding of resources that could benefit the poor or less fortunate. This self-centered drive ignores the needs of the vulnerable and widens the gap between the rich and the poor. From a moral standpoint, neglecting the duty to share and care for the less fortunate, belies the duty of "loving your neighbor." The Bible strongly condemns greed, warning of its destructive nature and spiritual consequences.

In 1 Timothy 6:10, it states, *"For the love of money is the root of evil,"* revealing how loving money over loving people leads individuals away from the faith and causes many sorrows. Proverbs

15:27 also warns that, *"He who is greedy of gain troubles his own house,"* explaining how greed brings strife and discord. Jesus also emphasizes this in Luke 12:15, saying, *"And he said unto them, Take heed, and beware of covetousness: for a man's life consisteth not in the abundance of the things which he possesseth."* This passage teaches that life's true value is not found in material possessions but in spiritual riches. The Bible consistently encourages contentment, generosity, and trust in God's provision, contrasting these virtues with the emptiness that greed brings. Accumulating things on earth will never fill a void. Material things provide only a brief and temporary pleasure, but eventually, that pleasure flees. Buying expensive houses, cars, bags, shoes or jewelry will not eradicate insecurity, depression, hurt, unfullfillment, or sadness; and eventually, all of those things will rot and have to be thrown away, even though they cost so much money. This is why we are warned in the Bible when it says in Mathew 6:19-21, *Laynot up for yourselves treasures upon earth, where moth and rust doth corrupt, and where thieves break through and steal.But lay up for yourselves treasures in heaven, where neither moth nor rust doth corrupt, and where thieves do not break through nor steal. For where your treasure is, there will your heart be also.*

Ahab's Entitled Greed

King Ahab was a wicked ruler in Israel. He possessed immense wealth, power, and authority. As king, there was very little he lacked. Yet, his heart was drawn to Naboth's vineyard, which was only a small plot of land that caught his eye. Despite having vast resources of the kingdom, Ahab wanted what belonged to Naboth, revealing his greed and covetous nature. When Naboth refused to sell the vineyard to him because it was an inheritance handed down to him from family, Ahab became disconcerted since he was not used to being denied anything by anyone. His wife, Queen Jezebel, seeing Ahab's distress, devised a wicked plan to falsely accuse Naboth of blasphemy. This led to Naboth's unjust execution. After Naboth died,

Ahab took the vineyard. However, Ahab's greed did not go unnoticed by God because God sees all.

Through the prophet Elijah, God pronounced judgment on Ahab and his family, declaring that disaster would fall upon his household, and that he would meet a violent death in the same place that Naboth was killed. This story serves as a powerful warning to each of us about the dangers of unchecked greed and/or desires for things (or people) that do not belong to us, and that are not rightfully ours to have. Even when we have much, greed can blind us to gratitude and integrity which can lead to destructive choices. The pursuit of more, at any cost, not only damages others but also brings about our own ruin. We must guard our hearts, find contentment in what we already have, and resist the urge to desire what belongs to others.

Generosity and greed stand in stark contrast, each shaping not only our actions but the condition of our hearts. Generosity opens doors, fosters relationships, and reflects a heart of compassion, mirroring the love of God. It brings joy, not just to the receiver, but to the giver and invites blessings, fulfillment, and spiritual growth. By giving freely, we align ourselves with the Divine principle that it is better to give than to receive. This creates a ripple effect of kindness and abundance. On the other hand, greed is a deceptive vice that promises satisfaction yet leaves a void that can never be filled. It drives individuals to pursue more without end, often at the expense of integrity, relationships, and spiritual well-being. Greed blinds us to the beauty of what we already have and hinders our ability to truly be grateful for them. Greed fosters discontent, isolates us from others and separates us from the joy of sharing.

As you read these words, I ask that you reflect on your own life. Are you nurturing a heart of generosity or succumbing to the allure of greed? True fulfillment comes not from possessing more but from sharing what

> *"Accumulating things on earth will never fill a void. Material things provide only a brief and temporary pleasure."*

you have. Cultivate the habit of giving, whether it's through kind words, time, resources, love or material blessings. Be vigilant of the desire for more, and when it becomes obsessive, pause and reassess. In choosing generosity over greed, you align yourself with a life of purpose, blessing, and genuine prosperity. Remember that it is not the abundance of possessions that defines a meaningful life, but the abundance of a generous heart. By practicing contentment and embracing a spirit of giving, you can break the cycle of greed and experience the blessings that come from a truly generous heart.

Lessons to Live By:

- Generosity embodies the moral excellence of giving freely without expecting anything in return and reveals kindness, empathy, and an open-hearted spirit.

- Generosity is seen as an act of faith, trusting that God will provide and multiply resources to meet your needs and the needs of others.

- Greed is an excessive desire to acquire or possess more than you need, particularly regarding material possessions, wealth or power.

- Greed is a deceptive vice that promises satisfaction yet leaves a void that can never be filled.

- Are you nurturing a heart of generosity or succumbing to the allure of greed?

15

Hope & Despair

Hope whispers of dawn where despair sees only night. Though despair may cloud the soul, hope renews vision, lifting the heart to believe in unseen light, reminding us that every dark season is temporary.

Hope is more than just a desire for better days. It is the constant flame that fuels resilience, the quiet strength that believes beyond what the eyes can see. Hope is the confident expectation of positive outcomes. It is a confident expectation that life can change for the better, even when present circumstances seem insurmountable. True hope doesn't only wish for improvement, it prepares, persists, and actively engages in the possibility of transformation. Hope combines optimism with intentionality and purpose. When you have the desire for a situation to turn around and the aspiration for something good to happen in the future, you have hope. Hope has confidence and belief in the possibility of a positive change or improvement despite how negative or discouraging the situation may be. A person demonstrates hope by maintaining a positive attitude and preparing for a positive transition. Being hopeful means having a mindset that trusts in potential of what can be even when you are faced with uncertainty or adversity. While optimism is having a general expectation of a positive outcome, hope combines that optimism with intentionality and a sense of purpose. Hope motivates you to continue moving forward, knowing that at any moment, despite what you may be in the midst of, things will change. To have hope is to expect good outcomes but also to actively pursue those outcomes. Hope carries an element of persistence and endurance.

Hope and faith are similar and are in the same family but are distinct. Hope is more about expecting positive outcomes in the future and has a desire or longing for a specific change or result. It keeps a person motivated and optimistic, especially during intense tests and trials. However, hope does not necessarily have a guaranteed assurance, but faith does. Faith has a stronger conviction. It involves a firm belief or trust, often without needing to see any tangible evidence. From a Christian perspective, faith is rooted in trust in God and His promises, regardless of what things look like from a natural perspective. While hope is often directed toward a specific outcome or desire, faith is anchored in a convictional trust, even when the outcome is unknown or unseen. Optimism alone may involve a general feeling that things will work out, but hope carries a more defined commitment to taking steps toward the expected outcome. It's fueled by both positive expectation and deliberate action, moving beyond passive waiting. For example, consider someone who is struggling with a health issue. Optimism might help them feel that their recovery is possible, but hope leads them to actively seek treatment, make lifestyle changes, and stick to their health plan. In this situation, their hope is not just about the desire to get better or wishing that it will, but it involves a purposeful effort rooted in a belief that their actions combined with a positive outlook, will bring about their desired change. This is where intentionality and purpose come into play, motivating the person to persist despite any setbacks and challenges.

Hope is a virtue because it reflects an inner strength that drives people toward good, even amid adversity. As a moral quality, it encourages resilience, perseverance, and cultivates a positive outlook that is rooted in a desire for a better future. Hope can shape one's character by emerging courage and tenacity, guiding them to act in alignment with their aspirations rather than giving in to despair or defeat. From a spiritual standpoint, hope connects us to a greater purpose and reinforces trust in God's promises, providing comfort and assurance that good can come from even the most trying circumstances. Hope is one of the pillars that serves as an anchor for the soul, instilling courage, lifting the spirit, and cultivating inner strength that helps us navigate life's uncertainties. Ultimately, hope makes life more meaningful because it nurtures our capacity to envision a better future.

Job's Hope

In the Bible, there is a story about a righteous man named Job found in the book called Job. Looking at his situation from the natural, he experienced sudden and severe suffering for no apparent reason. He lost his children, his possessions, his wealth, and also his health suddenly and unexpectantly. The story begins with Satan questioning Job's integrity before God, suggesting that his faithfulness to God was only because of his prosperity. In the story, God allowed Satan to test Job, who wrestled with the reason for all of his afflictions. However, despite his emotional, psychological and physical pain or how bad the situation in his life got, he consistently demonstrated hope in God's justice and sovereignty. Below are some examples that demonstrated how Job responded when confronted with one adversity after the next:

After losing his children, livestock, and servants in one day, Job's response was worship. His words reflected hope when he acknowledged God's sovereignty even in his immense grief.

1. *Then Job arose, and rent his mantle, and shaved his head, and fell down upon the ground, and worshipped, And said, Naked came I out of my mother's womb, and naked shall I return thither: the Lord gave, and the Lord hath taken away; blessed be the name of the Lord.* (Job 1:20-22)

2. When his wife urged him to curse God and die due to his physical suffering, Job's response demonstrated hope by trusting in God's control over both blessings and trials:

Thou speakest as one of the foolish women speaketh. What? shall we receive good at the hand of God, and shall we not receive evil?" In all this did not Job sin with his lips (Job 2:9-10).

3. When his friends accused him of sin, Job firmly declared hope in trusting in God. His statement of hope shows Job's unwavering trust in God's justice, even if it led to death.

Though he slay me, yet will I trust in him: but I will maintain mine own ways before him (Job 13:15).

4. Despite feeling abandoned, Job proclaimed,
For I know that my redeemer liveth, and that he shall stand at the latter day upon the earth: And though after my skin worms destroy this body, yet in my flesh shall I see God: Whom I shall see for myself, and mine eyes shall behold, and not another; though my reins be consumed within me." Here, Job's hope is evident in his confidence in a living Redeemer and the hope of resurrection (Job 19:25-27).

5. When defending his innocence, Job expressed hope, saying:

But he knoweth the way that I take: when he hath tried me, I shall come forth as gold." Job's words reflect hope that his trials will result in purification and vindication by God (Job 23:10).

6. After God responded to him from the whirlwind, revealing and reminding of His wisdom and dominion over creation, Job humbled himself, saying:

I have heard of thee by the hearing of the ear: but now mine eye seeth thee (Job 42:5).

God's response restored Job's hope, and ultimately, God blessed him with restored health, family, and wealth, confirming that his hope was rightly placed.

Throughout Job's trials, his hope was not impeccable, but it was resilient and was anchored in trust in God's character and ultimate justice, even when the reasons for his suffering were not fully revealed.

Job's story demonstrated that hope is not the absence of pain, but that in the midst of great suffering, we can still believe that we will come out of the situation and that it will not last forever. Job was confused, cried, and even questioned God, but his hope kept him from cursing his Maker or totally giving up, although many would have. Hope allows for honest expression of pain while maintaining a forward-looking faith that God is still at work, even in the midst of suffering and that in His own timing, He will work things out for our good. Throughout his trials, Job held on to his hope that God would eventually vindicate him. By the end, he not only had his fortune restored but he had also gained a deeper revelation of God's wisdom and majesty.

This story illustrated that hope can be a pathway to greater spiritual insight, as it keeps us seeking God even when we don't understand His ways. Job chose to trust God's nature, even when his emotions were overwhelmed by grief and despair, thus teaching that hope is a deliberate decision to keep faith operative, often in the absence of visible evidence or reassurance. True hope looks beyond temporary circumstances to the ultimate fulfillment of God's promises. God honors and rewards persistent hope, especially when it is grounded in faith and trust in His goodness. Ultimately, Job's story highlights that hope is a sustaining virtue, strengthening us to trust God's wisdom, timing, and redemptive plans, even in the darkest seasons.

Despair

The opposite of hope is despair, which is characterized by a sense of hopelessness, where we feel overwhelmed by negative thoughts and circumstances, causing us to believe that positive change is impossible. While hope gives the impetus towards acting with purpose and belief for better outcomes, despair leads to feelings of defeat, discouragement, and a lack of motivation to continue striving for good. Despair not only diminishes optimism but it also steals one's sense of purpose, resulting in apathy or discouragement. Despair weakens faith and disconnects a person from their sense of Divine connection or trust, making it a significant barrier to both spiritual and personal growth. Throughout biblical history, despair is seen whenever people turn from God and place their hope in temporary things that never satisfy them. Demonstratively, despair entered the world through humanity's initial rejection of God's will, leading to an ongoing struggle between good and evil, faith and doubt, hope and despair. However, the promise of redemption through Jesus Christ offers a way to overcome despair, restore hope and reconcile humanity back to God. Despair entered this world as a consequence of sin, beginning with the fall of Adam in the Garden of Eden. In Genesis 3, when Adam and Eve disobeyed God by eating from the Tree of the Knowledge of Good and Evil, suffering, separation from God, and ultimately death, entered the world because of sin and its effects. This disobedience not only brought physical and spiritual death but also a sense of loss, fear, and estrangement from God's presence, which are the roots of despair. The fall disrupted the perfect harmony that existed between humanity and God. Pain, toil, and brokenness were introduced. Despair arose, in addition to everything that is contrary to peace and good.

A person often reaches the point of despair when they are constantly and continuously faced with overwhelming difficulties, unresolved pain, or repeated setbacks that gradually erode their hope. Prolonged adversity, whether in relationships, health, finances, or personal failures, can create feelings of powerlessness. When attempts to overcome these challenges fail or seem futile, a sense of despair can emerge. Despair is a vice because it undermines your ability to persevere, trust, and seek redemption or positive change. It contributes to a mindset of defeat and leads to inaction, apathy, or even destructive behaviors. From a spiritual perspective, despair is very harmful because it contradicts trust in God's goodness, mercy, and His ability to intervene and correct the situation. Despair distances you from God's grace and replaces faith and hope with doubt and discouragement. Despair not only stifles spiritual growth but it can also diminish virtues such as courage, resilience, and faith, making it a barrier to living a fulfilling, virtuous life.

Overcoming Despair

Overcoming despair requires spiritual renewal, a mindset shift, and active engagement in life. Turning to God is essential, as it reestablishes trust in His promises, power, and love. Prayer, reading scripture, and seeking God's presence renews hope and provides comfort. Remembering and reading God's promises can reaffirm faith that God can transform despair into purpose. Ultimately, overcoming despair is a process that involves reliance on God, a shift in focus, and renewed engagement with life's possibilities. It's about choosing to hope and trust, even when it feels difficult, allowing God to bring healing and redemption.

Job's Despair

We explored how Job demonstrated hope while in the midst of his trials. Now, we will use Job's story to illustrate how even the most faithful can fall into despair. Job's journey shows both the depths of human anguish and how despair, though real and intense, can be overcome by God's mercy and justice. His despair began when he lost his wealth, health, and children one after the other. Before he could fully process one loss, another one came, then another, then another. Overcome by grief, he initially showed hope by worshipping God, but as his suffering persisted, he began to feel deep despair. In Job 3, he cursed the day of his birth, wishing he had never been born, saying, *"Let the day perish wherein I was born..."* (Job 3:3). This reveals how his pain led him to question his very existence. In *Job 6-7*, his despair deepens as he pleads for God to take his life. This revealed hopelessness and despair about his future: *"My days are swifter than a weaver's shuttle and are spent without hope"* (Job 7:6). He felt abandoned, as he cried, *"I will speak in the anguish of my spirit; I will complain in the bitterness of my soul"* (Job 7:11). Job's words illustrated how despair can consume a person, blinding them to God's presence and purpose, but even though one may fall in the valley of despair, they can always climb back up to hope, to faith and ultimately to victory. Job's story teaches us that even the strongest individuals can fall into despair, but despair does not have to be permanent. By staying close to God, even in the depths of his anguish, Job eventually found renewed hope and restoration. His experience highlighted that God's mercy, justice, and faithfulness will ultimately prevail and penetrate even the darkest despair and offer redemption to those who persevere through faith.

In both hope and despair, the story of Job teaches us a profound lesson about the human spirit. It is capable of enduring much, but only when anchored in God's unchanging character. Hope is not the absence of hardship, nor is despair the absence of faith, but rather, they are two responses to life's trials, one that propels us forward with expectation, and one that tempts us to retreat into hopelessness. Yet, as Job's journey demonstrates, even in our darkest moments, God's mercy and justice will always prevail. We may not always understand God's ways, but we can trust that His plans are good and will bring hope that transcend despair. Ultimately, despair can be transformed, not by our strength alone, but by God's sustaining grace. Let Job's story remind you that hope is always within reach, even in the bleakest seasons, and that God's redemptive power is able to restore, strengthen and make all things new.

Lessons to Live By:

- Hope is a confident expectation that life can change for the better, even when present circumstances seem insurmountable.

- While optimism is having a general expectation of a positive outcome, hope combines that optimism with intentionality and a sense of purpose.

- Despair not only diminishes optimism but it also steals one's sense of purpose, resulting in apathy or discouragement.

- Despair entered this world as a consequence of sin, beginning with the fall of Adam in the Garden of Eden.

- Hope is always within reach, even in the bleakest seasons.

16

Compassion & Apathy

Compassion moves the heart to care, bridging divides and healing wounds, while apathy turns away, as is indifferent to the needs of others. Embracing compassion enriches the soul, while apathy withholds the warmth that binds humanity.

When it comes to compassion and apathy, think about this: everyday, we are faced with choices that define our characters and shape our world. Compassion is a powerful force that calls us to be aware of the suffering that is around us and to respond with genuine care and action. It invites us to step outside of our own comfort zones and recognize the struggles of others, offering a helping hand and providing words of encouragement if needed. This benevolence provides a sense of connection to what others go through and helps us to realize that everyone's plight is different. This deep awareness often ignites a desire to alleviate the pain of those in need, prompting us to extend kindness and support, and to stand in solidarity with those who are hurting. In stark contrast, apathy represents a withdrawal from that level of concern. It is a state of indifference that causes one to overlook the challenges faced by others, leading to a lack of meaningful connection. Apathy can thrive in environments where pain and suffering are ignored, creating barriers to empathy and compassion. As we explore the dynamics between these two powerful approaches, we will uncover how cultivating compassion not only enriches our lives and the lives of others but also plays a vital role in creating a more caring and connected community.

Compassion is a deep awareness and caring for the suffering of others combined with a desire to alleviate that suffering. It involves a recognition of the struggles, hardships and pain that other people experience and feeling a genuine concern for their well-being. Compassion often leads to acts of kindness, support, and understanding, and it motivates people to help others in need. Compassion embodies empathy, which is the ability to understand and share in the feelings of another, but it also goes further by including a willingness to act in response to that understanding. Overall, compassion enriches both the lives of the one on the receiving end and the one who extends compassion through support. In the Old Testament, compassion is demonstrated in God's dealings with His people. For example, in Psalm 103:13, it states, *"As a father has compassion on his children, so the Lord has compassion on those who fear him."* In the New Testament, Jesus exemplifies compassion in His ministry. For example, in Matthew 9:36, it says, *"But when he saw the multitudes, he was moved with compassion on them, because they fainted, and were scattered abroad, as sheep having no shepherd."* This verse shows how empathetic and compassionate Jesus was and is for the struggles that people go through and His desire to help them.

The Good Samaritan

The story of The Good Samaritan is found in Luke 10:25-37. In this story, Jesus illustrates true compassion and what it means to "love your neighbor." In the story, a man who was traveling from Jerusalem to Jericho was stripped and attacked by a group of robbers. He was beaten and left half-dead. A priest who happened to be walking by, saw the injured man, but instead of helping him, he went to the other side of the road, choosing not to help. Shortly after the priest, a Levite, who belonged to the priestly tribe, also noticed the injured man but did the same thing the priest did and avoided involvement or assistance. Both of these "Men of God", despite their religious backgrounds, failed to demonstrate compassion, prioritizing their own convenience over the man's urgent need. Shortly thereafter, a Samaritan (a member of a group typically despised by the Jews) saw the wounded man. Unlike the last two, the Samaritan man was "moved by compassion" and tended to the injured man's wounds with oil and wine. He placed the man on his animal and took him to an inn for additional care. He even paid the innkeeper to continue caring for the wounded man and promised to cover any additional expenses that may be incurred while he was gone. The Samaritan's compassion was evident in his willingness to inconvenience himself, take risks, and spend his own resources to help a stranger in need. Unlike the priest and the Levite, the Samaritan's compassion transcended social barriers and demonstrated genuine mercy and compassion on someone in need. Jesus used this parable to emphasize that true compassion is active, sacrificial, and unbounded by societal divisions.

Background of the Samaritans

The Samaritans were a marginalized group of Jews who were looked down upon by other Jews as a lesser class due to historical, religious, and ethnic differences. The Jews disowned the Samaritans when they intermarried with foreign settlers after the Assyrian conquest of Israel (2 Kings 17). This led to their practices being seen as impure by the Jews when they blended cultures and religious practices with that of foreigners. Although they were also Jews, they were differentiated by being called "Samaritans" signifying that they were the Jews who intermarried with people from other conquered regions. The Jews went to great lengths to avoid the Samaritans and considered them spiritually inferior and socially unworthy. Despite this stigma, the good Samaritan in Jesus' parable showed a remarkable level of humanity and compassion, contrasting significantly with the behavior and inaction of the priest and the Levite, two men who were highly regarded in Jewish society. The compassion of the Samaritan man surpassed societal divisions and demonstrated that true humanity is not determined by social status or religious standing but by a heart willing to help others, regardless of their identity. Those so-called "upstanding citizens" were expected to uphold God's law by helping their neighbor, but they chose not to. In contrast, the Samaritan, often scorned, ridiculed and rejected by the Jewish community, embodied the essence of love and mercy. Jesus used this parable to highlight the irony: those who were viewed as spiritually superior failed to live out the very law of love they claimed to uphold, while the "lesser" Samaritan exemplified the highest form of moral and spiritual virtue. This story challenges the viewpoint of superiority, showing that compassion can emerge from unexpected places and that humanity is defined not by social class or religious identity, but by the capacity to love, serve, and care for others selflessly.

Apathy

Apathy is the opposite of compassion and is characterized by a lack of interest, care, or compassion regarding people and what they are going through. Apathy is often displayed as indifference, lack of concern or a disconnection from issues that most find important. Apathy is a vice because it stifles positive action, neglects involvement in addressing injustice, and perpetuates indifference toward the needs of others. Apathy can also prevent personal growth because it limits activity and engagement with the deeper, more meaningful aspects of life.

In looking at the same story you just read about from a different perspective, we can shift our focus from the compassion of the good Samaritan to the apathy of the priest who saw the injured man first. While the good Samaritan demonstrated compassion in action, the priest's behavior demonstrated a huge contrast that revealed the vice of apathy. Despite his role as a spiritual leader, one whose behavior should have embodied love and mercy, the priest chose to turn a blind eye to the wounded man's suffering. His indifference not only exposed a lack of empathy but it revealed a hypocrisy from the very person called to set the standard for compassion but failed to meet it.

> *"Apathy can thrive in environments where pain and suffering are ignored, creating barriers to empathy and compassion."*

Compassion at its core is about recognizing suffering and feeling compelled to alleviate it through active, selfless love. True compassion transcends social barriers and serves as a reflection of God's nature, promotes unity, understanding, and positive change. Apathy, on the other hand, is a barrier to compassion and action and blocks the flow of empathy and moral action. As seen in the priest's reaction in the parable, apathy not only reveals a lack of concern and uncaring attitude, but also exposes hypocrisy, particularly in those called to lead with love. God has called us as Christians to embrace compassion and recognize it as essential to moral and spiritual growth with an understanding that genuine humanity is defined by love in action, not by social status or title.

Lessons to Live By:

- Compassion often leads to acts of kindness, support, and understanding, and it motivates people to help others in need.

- Apathy is a vice because it reflects a lack of compassion, empathy, or active concern for the well-being of others.

- Apathy can also prevent personal growth, as it limits activity and engagement with the deeper, more meaningful aspects of life.

- Compassion enriches both the lives of the one on the receiving end and the one who extends compassion through support.

- Compassion at its core is about recognizing suffering and feeling compelled to alleviate it through active, selfless love.

17

Confidence & Insecurity

Confidence stands firm, embraces strengths and weaknesses alike, while insecurity doubts and hides from potential. Choosing confidence empowers growth and purpose, while insecurity clouds self-worth, holding us back from all we can become.

When it comes to confidence, let's consider the following two women. We will call them Angie and Kimberly. They are both beautiful, inside and out. Both are smart, educated, gifted, and talented. The skills they each possess are equal. However, Angie goes farther in life than Kimberly and embraces life with confidence and optimism. Angie has opportunities that Kimberly has never had. In their social lives, Angie has many friends while Kimberly has two close friends that she talks to ever so often. Angie is always approached by young men asking her out on dates, but Kimberly can count on one hand the number of dates she has had. She rarely gets asked out. The difference between these two women is that Angie embodies confidence while Kimberly grapples with insecurities. As we explore the complex interplay between confidence and insecurity, we will uncover how cultivating confidence can transform your life and open doors to success and fulfillment.

Confidence is a feeling of self-assurance that emerges from belief in one's value, qualities, and self-efficacy. It allows people to approach life with assurance and determination. Confidence compels one to act boldly, yet not aggressively and enables a person to take risks without being paralyzed by self-doubt. This inner strength manifests itself in assertive communication, assured body language, and a steady demeanor under pressure. A balanced confidence is assertiveness, not aggressiveness. The difference between the two lies in the approach and intent behind one's behavior. Assertiveness is characterized by clear and respectful communication of one's thoughts, feelings, and needs, while also considering the perspectives and viewpoints of others. A confident person expresses themselves firmly, standing their ground without belittling, overtalking or overpowering others. They engage in healthy and calm dialogue, seek compromise, and foster collaboration, valuing both their voice and those of others.

On the other hand, aggression often stems from a desire to mask insecurity or a need for control. An aggressive person may resort to hostility, intimidation, or dismissive behavior to assert their dominance or validate their position. This can create conflict and alienate others because it prioritizes one's own needs at the expense of mutual respect and understanding. In contrast, the opposite of confidence is insecurity or self-doubt. Insecurity involves a lack of faith in one's abilities, qualities, or skillset, often resulting in hesitation, fear of failure, and an overall sense of inadequacy. This perception of oneself can limit personal growth, hinder decision-making, and create feelings of hesitancy or uncertainty in various situations.

Confidence is an internal state that manifests itself through behavior that reflects trust in one's capacity to succeed or handle challenges. It allows people to act boldly, take risks, and make decisions without excessive doubt or fear. Confidence is a virtue because it fosters personal growth and development and propels one to pursue challenging, yet realistic goals that are aligned to one's skillsets. Confidence inspires trust in others, as confident people often lead by example and uplift those around them. Confidence encompasses several core elements as delineated below:

1. **Belief in One's Abilities:** Confidence involves a strong embrace of one's skills, strengths, and efficacy. It's about

knowing what your personal strengths are while also being aware of areas for improvement.

2. **Resilience**: Confidence embodies self-assuredness even in the face of setbacks. Confident people are often resilient and able to navigate challenges or failures without feeling defeated. This resilience fuels the willingness to try again and learn from mistakes and adapt.

3. **Positive Self-Perception**: Confidence is deeply rooted in how one perceives themselves. It involves having a healthy level of self-esteem, where you feel that you are worthy and have value without arrogance, superiority, or overestimation.

4. **Clear Communication**: Confidence is displayed through clear and assertive communication. This involves speaking directly, maintaining eye contact, and engaging in conversations with clarity and conviction. Confident people tend to express their thoughts clearly without hesitance or self-doubt.

5. **Body Language**: Body Language speaks loud and clearly! It is visibly displayed through the way you walk, sit, stand, enter a room, the way you posture, your handshake, and steady eye contact. These non-verbal cues reflect internal confidence, making others perceive you as self-assured.

6. **Calm Under Pressure**: Confidence allows you to remain calm and collected, especially in stressful or unfamiliar situations. Confident people are able to think logically, stay composed, and make decisions without being easily swayed by fear or anxiety.

Confidence is more than just a feeling; it is a mindset that shapes behaviors, interactions, and overall self-perception. It empowers you to pursue your written goals and navigate around challenges and foster healthier relationships with yourself and others.

Overconfidence

Overconfidence is an excessive belief in one's abilities or judgment, often exceeding actual capability or efficacy. Overconfidence can lead to risky decisions and can underestimate situations and people while ignoring potential mistakes. While it can drive bold actions and persistence, overconfidence is generally considered negative because it can result in poor decision-making and failure to learn from errors. Overconfidence can also cause strained relationships due to arrogance or dismissiveness.

David's Impressive Confidence

David, a young shepherd boy, displayed unwavering confidence in God when he faced the giant Goliath. Despite his youth and inexperience in battle, he declared victory even before the fight began because he trusted in God rather than expressing faith in his weapons. His confidence in God allowed him to defeat Goliath with a single stone, which elevated him to a national hero and lead to his eventual rise as king of Israel. Confidence can propel you forward in life by allowing you to embrace opportunities and creating a pathway for elevation. It creates a positive impression, making others more likely to trust, collaborate, and offer you greater roles or responsibilities. Confidence enables you to take calculated risks, overcome failures, and persist in achieving your goals, which is essential for success.

Insecurity

Insecurity is a feeling of self-doubt or lack of confidence in oneself, often stemming from comparison to others or fear of failure. This trait can hinder personal progress because it creates a barrier to taking risks and prevents you from seeking out premier opportunities. Insecure people most times avoid situations where they fear being judged or rejected. Insecurity is not a desirable trait because it subverts the potential for growth, fulfillment, and overall well-being, perpetuating a cycle of self-doubt and stagnation. Despite having gifts, talents, and skills, a person may still experience insecurity due to past negative experiences, such as criticism or failure, which may have instilled a fear of inadequacy. Comparisons with others can also exacerbate feelings of insecurity, especially in competitive environments where people feel they do not measure up to others. Low self-esteem and a negative self-image contribute to insecurity because individuals may struggle to recognize their worth despite their abilities.

External pressures, such as societal expectations or the desire for approval from others, can create anxiety and self-doubt which can overshadow one's talents. Insecurity is a vice rather than a virtue because it can lead to detrimental behaviors and unhealthy thought patterns that can negatively impact an individual's life. Unlike virtues that promote positive qualities and constructive actions, insecurity feeds self-doubt, fear, and avoidance which hinders personal growth and the pursuit of opportunities. This vice can also contribute to a cycle of negativity, where fear of failure or fear of rejection prevent insecure people from fully embracing their potential or expressing their talents. In contrast, virtues encourage resilience, self-acceptance, and proactive engagement with life's challenges. This fosters a healthier mindset and overall well-being.

Gideon's Insecurity

Gideon's story is set during a time of turmoil for the Israelites, who were oppressed by the Midianites. The Midianites invaded Israel, destroyed their crops, and took their livestock, which left the Israelites in fear and desperation. In response to their cries for help, God chose Gideon to lead a rebellion against the Midianites and deliver them from oppression. However, Gideon's insecurity was clearly revealed when he encountered the angel of the Lord who called him a "mighty warrior" and gave him the charge to "save" Israel. Initially, Gideon expressed insecurity about his capabilities, pointing out his family's low social status in Manasseh and his own insignificance. He questioned why God had allowed Israel to suffer and looked for confirmation of his calling by asking for miraculous signs. For instance, he requested that a fleece be wet with dew while the ground remained dry and then reversed the request by asking that the fleece remain dry while the ground around it was wet with dew. Despite doubts about whether he was actually called to deliver Israel, Gideon was able to overcome his insecurities through a series of Divine encounters and confirmations. God reassured him that he was the one that God had chosen for the task and provided signs that affirmed his role as leader.

Gideon gathered an army, but God instructed him to reduce the numbers to only 300 men. The purpose of this was for God to show them that victory would come through His power rather than human strength. Gideon's obedience and faith led to a great and surprising victory over the Midianites. This victory revealed that by trusting God and stepping out in faith, one could transcend their insecurities and fulfill their Divine calling. This transformation not only empowered Gideon but also served as a pivotal moment in Israel's history.

Angie and Kimberly

Now let's go back to the story of the two women from the opening of this chapter. Remember that Angie and Kimberly were equal in beauty, gifts, talents and skillsets. The only difference between them was in their self-image and confidence levels. Angie's confidence propelled her to great heights in every area of her life, while Kimberly's insecurities prevented her from pursuing meaningful goals, taking risks or embracing great opportunities when they were presented to her. The contrast between these two women lied in their mindsets. While Kimberly possessed similar abilities and qualities as Angie, her insecurity manifested as self-doubt and fear of rejection. This led to hesitance and reluctance to engage fully in social situations, and an overly cautious approach to dating. Consequently, her potential remained unrealized and unrecognized, and she often missed out on the same opportunities that her confident counterpart embraced. Ultimately, Angie's belief in herself and her willingness to take calculated risks propelled her forward in ways that could feel elusive to those who struggle with insecurity, like Kimberly.

In her professional life, Angie's confidence was palpable. She approached challenges with a proactive mindset and embraced opportunities for growth and advancement. Angie spoke up respectfully and calmly in meetings, shared her ideas with clarity, and took initiative on projects, thus showcasing belief in herself and her abilities. Her coworkers and superiors respected her not only for her skills but also for her assertive, yet professional demeanor. She actively sought out mentorships and networking opportunities, understanding that building relationships is essential for career progression. As a result, Angie often found herself considered for promotions or special projects, which led her to achieving significant goals that others did not often reach. Angie's name was often spoken about favorably when she was not around, and her name was synonymous with hard work, integrity and confidence.

In contrast, Kimberly, though equally talented and capable, struggled with insecurity in her professional life. She often hesitated to voice her ideas in meetings, fearing judgment or rejection from her colleagues. While she had valuable insights, she tended to remain quiet, missing out on opportunities to highlight her expertise. More often than not, Kimberly refused to share great ideas that would come to her mind and later down the line, someone else would articulate the exact same idea that Kimbely first conceived, but the person who shared it with the team was praised and rewarded for it when it was executed. Kimberly often found herself overthinking about her contributions and often focused on what she perceived as her shortcomings rather than recognizing and embracing her strengths. Although she worked hard and met deadlines, she often felt overlooked and underappreciated, which reinforced her insecurities. In her efforts to connect with others, she came across as uncertain or overly accommodating, which made it difficult for her to assert her needs or seek out mentorship. Consequently, Kimberly found it challenging to advance in her career, often watching people like Angie seize opportunities that she felt she was just as deserving of. Confidence bridges the gap between potential and achievement, because it gives you the impetus to step out on faith and pursue those opportunities with optimism and faith. Confidence allows you to showcase your skills to the world, while a lack of confidence can often keep talents unnoticed or underutilized.

From a social standpoint, Angie's confidence shined brightly in her ability to connect with people. She engaged in conversations with ease and maintained eye contact and body language that invited others in. Friends were drawn to her magnetic personality, and they appreciated her positive outlook and willingness to support them. Because she was comfortable in her own skin, Angie fostered authentic relationships and created a strong support network. Her confidence encouraged her to seek new experiences, such as joining organizations, participating in community events, sitting on boards or traveling. Through these, she was able to meet a diverse range of people and expand her social circle. In contrast, Kimberly's insecurities significantly impacted her social life. While she longed for connections, she often felt apprehensive in social situations, second-guessing herself and fearing how others perceived her. As a result, she avoided initiating conversations or engaging fully, often choosing to listen rather than share her own thoughts or experiences. This hesitance led her to feel isolated, even in group settings because she struggled to express herself and connect on a deeper level. Kimberly's tendency to compare herself to others and their accomplishments further fed her feelings of inadequacy and made her retreat from opportunities to socialize or participate in new activities. Ultimately, while Angie thrived in her social life, and embraced her confidence to foster meaningful connections, Kimberly found herself grappling with self-doubt and missing out on the vibrant experiences and friendships that could have enriched her life.

In her dating life, Angie approaches relationships with a healthy sense of self-worth. She knows what she brings to the table and is not afraid to express her desires and boundaries. This self-assuredness allows her to engage in dating with openness while seeking partners who appreciate her for who she is and what she brings to the table. Angie views relationships as opportunities for growth rather than validations of her worth, which empowers her to bond with companions that she likes based on mutual respect and understanding. Her confidence naturally attracts potential partners; as they are drawn to her authenticity and the joy she exudes. Even when faced with rejection or challenges, she handles them gracefully, viewing the experiences as part of her personal journey rather than personal failures.

In stark contrast, Kimberly's insecurities profoundly affect her dating life. While she yearns for companionship and love, her self-doubt often holds her back from pursuing meaningful connections. In social settings, men perceive her hesitation and uncertainty, which can lead to them treating her dismissively or with less respect. Insecure women like Kimberly may feel pressure to seek validation from their partners, which can create a dynamic where they compromise their own needs and boundaries. This behavior not only undermines her self-esteem but also makes her more vulnerable to mistreatment.

Men can "sense" or "smell" insecurity in women like Kimberly and unfortunately, this can attract the wrong kind of attention. Men who are less genuine may exploit the insecurities in these types of women. They might take advantage of their fears of rejection and abandonment, dismiss their feelings, or belittle their concerns, reinforcing their negative self-image. As a result, Kimberly finds herself in unfulfilling relationships where she feels undervalued and overlooked. While Angie flourishes in her dating life, cultivating connections that uplift and inspire her, Kimberly struggles to break free from the cycle of insecurity and mistreatment, longing for the same authentic love that her confident counterpart effortlessly attracts.

For the reasons outline in this chapter, embracing confidence in who you are, what you bring to the table and your self-worth is pivotal in every area

> *"Confidence is more than just a feeling; it is a mindset that shapes behaviors, interactions, and overall self-perception."*

of life. Building confidence is a transformative journey for an insecure person, and it often begins with recognizing and addressing the underlying insecurities that hold them back. By taking intentional steps, individuals can gradually cultivate self-assurance and a more positive self-perception. Just remember, confidence is a virtue. Insecurity is a vice.

Lessons to Live By:

- Confidence is a powerful feeling of self-assurance that emerges from a belief in one's abilities, qualities, and self-efficacy.

- Assertiveness is characterized by clear and respectful communication of one's thoughts, feelings, and needs while also considering the perspectives and viewpoints of others.

- Confidence is more than just a feeling; it is a mindset that shapes behaviors, interactions, and overall self-perception.

- Insecurity involves a lack of faith in one's abilities, qualities, or skillset, often resulting in hesitation, fear of failure, and an overall sense of inadequacy.

- Comparisons with others can also exacerbate feelings of insecurity, especially in competitive environments where people feel they do not measure up.

18

Kindness & Cruelty

Kindness nurtures and uplifts the soul, leaving a energy of warmth and connection, while cruelty wounds and divides, sowing seeds of pain. Choosing kindness shapes a world of light, while cruelty darkens the spirit within and around us.

Kindness and cruelty are two opposite forces that significantly shape human interactions and societal dynamics. Kindness creates bonds, empathy, and understanding. It creates an environment where people feel valued and supported. It has the power to heal, uplift, and inspire positive change. In contrast, cruelty undermines trust, inflicts harm, and perpetuates cycles of pain and division. Acts of cruelty can have far-reaching consequences, affecting not only the victims of it, but also the inflictors. Kindness brings light to even the darkest days, illuminating our interactions with peace and compassion. When we engage in acts of kindness, whether through a simple compliment, a helping hand, or a listening ear, we create moments of positivity that uplift not only the recipient but also ourselves. Choosing kindness can enrich our lives and the lives of others, promoting an environment where empathy and understanding flourish.

Kindness is the quality of being friendly, generous, or considerate toward others. It involves some of the other virtues discussed in this book, such as compassion, empathy, hope, peace and courtesy. Being kind should be practiced daily because it fosters positive relationships and creates a culture of morale and motivation. Kindness improves emotional well-being for both the giver and the receiver. It also makes our environments whether at home, work, or

"

in public, more pleasant and peaceful. A simple kind gesture can have a profound impact on someone's life by uplifting their spirits or providing comfort and reassurance during challenging times. We can never know the impact that a kind gesture can have on someone's life. A simple compliment, smile, or action of support can make the difference between life or death for someone considering taking their own life. Such acts can foster a sense of acceptance, belonging, and connection, making individuals feel valued and appreciated. For someone facing difficulties, a kind gesture may restore hope and motivate them to persevere. Moreover, kindness can encourage positive behavior and inspire others to go over and beyond or pay it forward, thus creating a cycle of goodwill. Kindness and courtesy are closely related although they have slight nuances. There is a saying that kindness and courtesy can take one farther than money can. Kindness builds trust and goodwill that money alone cannot do. It enhances one's reputation and encourages others to support them as well. Ultimately, while money can offer immediate benefits, kindness creates lasting impacts, contributing to personal fulfillment and a positive legacy that extends beyond financial resources.

From an early age, I instilled in my son the importance of kindness, compassion, and empathy towards people. I made sure he understood that many people did not have some of the privileges he enjoyed, whether due to financial constraints or otherwise. As an educator of students with special needs at one point, I taught him about children who have disabilities and how we are to show compassion and have empathy towards them. I also taught him how to display kindness in social settings and encouraged him to recognize moments where he could make a difference in someone's life through a kind gesture. I taught him to approach people with respect and warmth, even those who might not fit societal standards of beauty. I advised him that when he encountered any young lady who may be considered less attractive or bigger than the average by social standards, to greet them by saying, *"Good morning beautiful."* A small greeting such as that could significantly uplift her spirits. As of this writing, (November 2024), my son is 26 years old and he still practices this small, but powerful act of kindness. It costs nothing to be kind, but the rewards in boosting someone's self-worth can be immeasurable. Over time, a reputation for being kind can lead to greater respect and admiration from others. As a virtue, kindness encourages individuals to act for the greater good rather than merely pursuing personal interests. Kindness aligns with many ethical and philosophical teachings that emphasize the importance of treating others with respect and dignity. Below are five scriptures that talk about the importance of being kind:

1. **Ephesians 4:32**: And be ye kind one to another, tenderhearted, forgiving one another, even as God for Christ's sake hath forgiven you.

2. **Proverbs 11:17**: "The merciful man doeth good to his own soul: but he that is cruel troubleth his own flesh."

3. **Colossians 3:12**: "Put on therefore, as the elect of God, holy and beloved, bowels of mercies, kindness, humbleness of mind, meekness, longsuffering."

4. **Galatians 6:10**: "As we have therefore opportunity, let us do good unto all men, especially unto them who are of the household of faith."

5. **Titus 3:4-5**: "But after that the kindness and love of God our Savior toward man appeared, not by works of righteousness which we have done, but according to his mercy he saved us, by the washing of regeneration, and renewing of the Holy Ghost."

The Shunamite Woman

The story of the Shunamite woman, found in 2 Kings 4:8-37, exemplifies kindness through one woman's hospitality and generosity toward the prophet Elisha. She recognized him as a man of God who passed through her town often, so she decided to extend kindness by inviting him to her home for a meal. Her kindness did not stop there either. She and her husband prepared a small room for him, with a bed, a table, a chair, and a lamp. This act of hospitality showed her deep respect and appreciation for his work as a prophet. The motivation behind her kindness toward Elisha was rooted in her recognition of his Divine calling and her desire to support God's work. In return for her generosity, God blessed her with a son as prophesied by the man of God, reflecting the biblical principle that acts of kindness can yield unexpected blessings. Her story illustrated how kindness can bring about blessings and foster Divine connections.

Cruelty

Cruelty is the intentional infliction of pain, suffering, or distress on others. It is often characterized by a lack of empathy or regard for the well-being of people. It can manifest in various forms, including physical violence, emotional abuse, or psychological manipulation. Cruelty can occur in interpersonal relationships, societal interactions, or broader contexts, such as systemic injustices. It reflects a disregard for human dignity and can lead to long-lasting harm, not only to victims but also to perpetrators and communities. Cruelty subverts trust, compassion, and the potential for healthy connections among people.

Kindness and cruelty are diametrically opposite in both intent and impact. Kindness is characterized by a genuine desire to uplift and support others. It creates an environment where individuals feel valued and understood. On the contrary, cruelty is defined by the intentional infliction of pain, suffering, or humiliation on others. It arises from a lack of empathy and often seeks to exert power or control, leading to emotional and physical harm. While kindness builds trust and strengthens relationships, cruelty erodes connections and creates division, leaving lasting scars. Kindness cultivates a sense of community and compassion, but cruelty perpetuates cycles of pain and disconnection.

The Rape of David's Daughter, Tamar

The rape of Tamar, as recounted in 2 Samuel 13, is a poignant example of cruelty that had far-reaching consequences. This story involved three of David's children: Tamar, Amnon and Absolom. Tamar, the beautiful daughter of King David, was brutally assaulted by her half-brother Amnon, who was driven by his obsessive lust. This horrible act not only violated Tamar's innocence but also devastated her emotionally and socially, as she faced shame and ostracism in a patriarchal society that often silenced victims. The cruelty of Amnon's actions set off a chain reaction of violence and revenge within King David's family. Tamar's brother Absalom was infuriated because he felt that there was no consequence against Amnon for what he had done to Tamar. Absolom, filled with rage, sought justice for his sister and ultimately murdered Amnon two years later during a feast. This cycle of cruelty and vengeance not only tore apart family bonds within King David's family, but it also led to Absalom's rebellion against his father. That act of violence against Tamar bred an environment where cruelty begot cruelty and highlighted the devastating impact of unchecked sin and the importance of addressing such acts with justice and compassion.

While some may argue that in a situation such as that one, cruelty served as a form of justice or retribution, the reality is that cruelty for cruelty rarely leads to positive outcomes. Cruelty typically perpetuates cycles of pain, resentment, and further violence, undermining the possibility of healing and reconciliation. Even if an individual is perceived as deserving of harsh treatment, responding with cruelty often escalates the situation, making it worse and can create lasting harm, both to the victim and the perpetrator. Literature, art, and media portrayals of cruelty can also significantly influence societal attitudes by shaping perceptions and emotional responses. Recognizing the profound impact of both kindness and cruelty emphasizes the importance of choosing compassion in our daily lives. By promoting kindness and addressing the roots of cruelty, we can cultivate a more empathetic and harmonious world where the transformative power of kindness prevails over the destructive nature of cruelty. Ultimately, our choices shape the fabric of our communities, making it vital to nurture kindness and challenge cruelty wherever it appears.

Lessons to Live By:

- Kindness fosters bonds, empathy, and understanding. It creates an environment where people feel valued and supported.

- We can never know the impact that a kind gesture can have on someone's life. A simple compliment, smile or action of support can make the difference between life or death for someone considering taking their own life.

- Cruelty can occur in interpersonal relationships, societal interactions, or broader contexts, such as systemic injustices. It reflects a disregard for human dignity and can lead to long-lasting harm.

- Cruelty typically perpetuates cycles of pain, resentment, and further violence, undermining the possibility of healing and reconciliation.

- Recognizing the profound impact of both kindness and cruelty emphasizes the importance of choosing compassion in our daily lives.

19

Peace & Turmoil

Peace brings stillness to the soul and grounds us in resilience and clarity, while turmoil stirs chaos, unsettling the heart. Embracing peace fosters harmony and strength, while turmoil drains our spirit and clouds our path.

Peace is one of life's greatest blessings. It is a sanctuary in the midst of chaos. In contrast to turmoil, whether emotional, mental, physical, financial, or spiritual, peace provides a profound sense of stability and well-being. Peace is the absence of conflict, stress, and disturbance. It includes both inner calmness and external calmness. It is only through experiencing the depths of turmoil that we can truly appreciate the tranquility that peace offers. Turmoil can manifest as relentless stress, inner conflict, or external strife that cast shadows over our lives and clouds our judgment. In those moments, peace can feel like a distant dream. This chapter will explore how peace serves as a vital virtue that fosters harmony. Peace is considered a virtue because it embodies qualities such as harmony, calmness, solitude, and understanding. It promotes emotional well-being and fosters positive relationships that encourage individuals to seek resolutions to conflicts rather than perpetuating cycles of confrontation, discord or violence.

As a virtue, peace inspires people to act with kindness and empathy and creates an environment where cooperation and mutual respect can flourish. Additionally, peace opens the door to personal growth and reflection because it enables people and communities to thrive without the burdens of fear and anxiety. Peace promotes a sense of safety and fosters constructive relationships and cooperation among people. It is often associated with emotional well-being, self-awareness, clarity of thought, and a positive outlook on life. Ultimately, peace fosters an environment where growth, collaboration, and mutual respect can flourish.

Peace can manifest in various forms, starting with individual peace, which is characterized by self-awareness and practices such as meditation, reading, prayer and mindfulness. In a household, peace is cultivated through open communication and mutual respect among family members, which creates a harmonious living environment. At the community level, peace develops through collaboration and effective conflict resolution among diverse groups, promoting understanding and cooperation. On a national scale, peace begins with governance that prioritizes justice and the protection of human rights. Each of these levels reinforces the importance of nurturing peace both individually and collectively.

Turmoil

The opposite of peace is turmoil. Turmoil is characterized by chaos, conflict, and disturbance. It manifests as internal unrest, emotional instability, or external strife within relationships, communities, or nations. Turmoil often involves feelings of anxiety, fear, and insecurity. These elements disrupt and disturb peace and harmony. Turmoil can arise from unresolved conflicts, societal injustice, or personal struggles, leading to a breakdown in communication and trust. Ultimately, turmoil undermines well-being and prevents individuals and groups from thriving. It can manifest in various forms, each affecting people and communities in different ways. Below are different kinds of turmoil:

1. **Emotional Turmoil**: This involves intense feelings of anxiety, sadness, or confusion, often stemming from unresolved issues, trauma, or relationship conflicts. It can disrupt a person's mental health and overall well-being.

2. **Mental Turmoil**: This is characterized by chaotic and negative thinking, stress, or cognitive dissonance. Mental

turmoil can hinder decision-making and clarity. It may result from overwhelming responsibilities, trauma, injustice, or persistent worry.

3. **Physical Turmoil**: This refers to disturbances in the body that can arise from illness, injury, or chronic pain that impacts a person's ability to function normally, affecting their overall quality of life. When the body experiences immense pain, the physical turmoil can be too much to bear, causing great emotional and psychological turmoil as well.

4. **Financial Turmoil**: This type of turmoil happens when individuals or families are faced with financial instability or hardship, such as job loss, overwhelming debt, or unexpected expenses. This can lead to stress and anxiety about meeting basic needs.

5. **Social Turmoil**: This encompasses conflicts within communities or society at large, such as political unrest, protests, or social injustice, which can disrupt social harmony and lead to violence or division.

6. **Spiritual Turmoil**: This involves a crisis of faith or a deep sense of spiritual disconnection, often prompting individuals to question their beliefs, purpose, or place in the world.

Each type of turmoil can significantly impact a person's life, emphasizing the importance of seeking peace and resolution in various areas of existence.

King David's Reign

From a biblical perspective, King David's reign was marked by significant turmoil, both personally and within his household. He initially faced internal strife emanating from the betrayal of his predecessor Saul who tried to kill him out of jealousy before he became king. After David became king, the traumatic events during his reign included the loss of his infant son with Bathsheba, which weighed heavily on him and symbolized the consequences of his sin. Additionally, his daughter Tamar was brutally raped by her own half-brother Amnon, and David's failure as a father regarding how he handled that situation led to the rebellion and betrayal of his son and Tamar's brother Absalom. All of this turmoil during his reign highlighted the deep-seated issues within his family, resulting in a legacy overshadowed by suffering and discord.

Solomon's Reign

In contrast, Solomon, David's son, experienced a reign marked by peace and prosperity. His rule is often depicted as a time of wisdom, wealth, and architectural advancement, including the construction of the Temple in Jerusalem. Solomon's wisdom, which was granted by God, allowed him to govern prudently. Unlike his father King David, Solomon's reign lacked turmoil, and his focus was on building and maintaining peace.

The dichotomy between David and Solomon illustrates how personal choices and familial dynamics can shape leadership and legacy. While David's reign was marked by the repercussions of sin and family conflict, Solomon's peace can be seen as a Divine blessing resulting from his commitment to wisdom and governance. However, it's important to note that Solomon's peace was not without its own challenges. His later years were troubled by his own disobedience and idolatry, which foreshadowed the eventual division of the kingdom. The concepts of peace and turmoil represent two contrasting states that significantly impact lives and communities. The interplay between peace and turmoil underscores the importance of cultivating an environment where peace can thrive. While turmoil can arise from personal, family, or societal challenges, the choice to seek peace through compassion, understanding, and effective conflict resolution can transform lives and communities. Ultimately, recognizing the value of peace encourages people to strive for harmony in their own lives and in the world around them.

- Peace is the absence of conflict, stress, and disturbance. It includes both inner calmness and external calmness.

- In a household, peace is cultivated through open communication and mutual respect among family members, which creates a harmonious living environment.

- The opposite of peace is turmoil, characterized by chaos, conflict, and disturbance.

- Peace is characterized by tranquility, harmony, and a sense of well-being that fosters positive relationships and emotional resilience.

- The interplay between peace and turmoil underscores the importance of cultivating an environment where peace can thrive.

20

Courtesy & Rudeness

Courtesy reflects respect and grace, fostering harmony and connection, while rudeness dismisses others and breeds division and discord. Choosing courtesy uplifts and honors, while rudeness diminishes both the giver and the receiver.

To be courteous is to display polite behavior and kind actions toward others. It includes showing respect, kindness, and thoughtfulness while interacting with others. Courtesy can be shown through simple words such as "please" and "thank you," the most basic, yet kind words in the human language. Courtesy reflects a person's character and fosters harmonious relationships. It also promotes understanding and cooperation, which contributes to a positive social environment that encourages people to put the needs of others before their own. Courtesy is aligned with good manners as both involve respectful and considerate behavior in social settings and interactions. Good manners include specific behaviors and etiquette that promote polite communication and graceful interactions, such as greeting others, using kind language, and observing social norms. Good manners are the formal expressions of courtesy. One's ability to connect with others through kindness and empathy often draws people to them, which enhances their social presence and reputation. Being courteous can actually calm the anger or agitation of someone by demonstrating respect and understanding. Polite and considerate communication can help defuse tension, as it shows the other person that their feelings are acknowledged and valued.

Courteous behavior, such as maintaining a calm tone, actively listening, and validating the concerns of another person, creates a more positive interaction. This strategic approach can shift the focus from conflict to resolution, making it easier for an agitated or angry person to feel heard and more willing to engage calmly. Ultimately, courtesy can foster a sense of safety and respect, reduce hostility and promote a peaceful atmosphere. When someone responds to rudeness with politeness and respect, it can disarm the rude behavior and potentially lead to a shift in the other person's attitude. Courteous interactions may also prompt the rude individual to reconsider their actions, feel a sense of shame, or realize the impact of their behavior. This approach can create an opportunity for more open and constructive communication and may encourage the rude person to adopt a more respectful demeanor. Ultimately, courtesy can serve as a powerful tool for influencing positive change in interpersonal dynamics.

A person who deliberately works at embracing courtesy in most interactions is self-aware and typically perceived as respectful, and kind. Others often view them as approachable and easy to engage with, which strengthens trust. Consistent politeness and consideration for the feelings of others enables others to perceive you as one who cares about humanity, thus creating a positive reputation for you. People are more likely to appreciate and respond positively to someone who exemplifies courtesy. It is important to point out that courtesy is not a sign of weakness; rather, it reflects strength of character and emotional intelligence, especially when it is directed towards those who are not the kindest or those who are typically agitated. Courtesy reveals self-control, confidence, and the ability to empathize with others. A courteous person can navigate challenging situations with grace, defuse tension and foster positive interactions. This strength can lead to more effective problem-solving, communication and better relationships, showcasing resilience and the ability to prioritize respect over conflict.

Being courteous and having good manners doesn't always require knowing the formal rules of etiquette. Courtesy comes from a genuine respect and kindness toward others, which can be shown through simple actions such as giving a greeting when you enter a room, listening attentively without interrupting when others are speaking, or helping someone in need. Even without knowing specific etiquette rules, one can demonstrate thoughtful consideration by being aware of the feelings of others and responding with empathy and respect. On the other hand, someone can possess knowledge of etiquette but still be rude, using politeness as a facade rather than a genuine expression of respect. Conversely, a person who knows all the etiquette rules can still be kind and courteous by applying those rules with a heart of generosity and sincerity, ensuring their actions are rooted in a desire to make others feel valued. Ultimately, kindness and courtesy are choices that anyone can adopt, regardless of their understanding of etiquette. It is a decision to treat others with dignity and care, and it can be practiced daily by anyone who truly desires to display respect and kindness in their interactions.

When we treat others with kindness, we not only uplift their spirits but also create opportunities for deeper connections. This approach can lead to unexpected encounters where the person on the kindness receiving end may turn out to be someone who plays a vital role in our lives, whether personally or professionally. When we act with kindness, we set a tone that encourages others to respond in kind, fostering a reciprocal cycle of goodwill. This can create a supportive network where people are more inclined to offer assistance or protection in times of need.

Abraham and his Three Visitors

The story of Abraham and the three visitors, found in Genesis 18:1-8, takes place at Abraham's tent in the plains of Mamre after God had established a covenant with him, promising that he would be the father of many nations. The three visitors, (later understood to be Divine angels), came to deliver two messages: 1.) that Abraham and Sarah would have a son despite being old, and 2.) to reveal God's impending judgment on Sodom and Gomorrah. Abraham extended courtesy to the visitors out of a deep sense of hospitality, which was a cultural norm in ancient Eastern society back then. He invited them to rest, provided water to wash their feet, and instructed his servant to prepare a meal for them. Through these acts, Abraham honored the visitors and demonstrated his courtesy and willingness to serve others, embodying the values of politeness, hospitality, and respect. At first, Abraham did not know the true identity of the three visitors. He greeted them as travelers and extended his hospitality without any indication that he knew that they were angels sent by God. It was only later in his conversation with them, when they revealed God's promise about Sarah giving birth to a son, that the extraordinary nature of their visit became clear.

Abraham's initial sincere courtesy reflected his graciousness and respect for guests, regardless of their identity. The lesson learned in this story is that being courteous to others, regardless of their identity, is a powerful practice that can lead to unexpected blessings and protection. As previously stated, acts of courtesy can sometimes yield unexpected blessings. For example, someone we assist or show kindness to may later provide us with invaluable support, opportunities, or connections we never anticipated. These blessings often arise from the relationships that are built on mutual respect and kindness, reinforcing the idea that our actions toward others can return to us in meaningful ways.

Rudeness

The antithesis of courtesy is rudeness. To be rude is to behave in a disrespectful, impolite, or inconsiderate manner toward others. This can manifest through harsh or offensive language, dismissive attitudes, or neglecting social etiquette. Rudeness often disregards the feelings and needs of others, leading to discomfort or awkwardness in interactions. It reflects a lack of consideration for social norms, can damage relationships and breeds rudeness, negativity and hostility. Rude people are often perceived as inconsiderate, untrustworthy, and lacking empathy and self-awareness. Their behavior can lead others to view them as having no class, uncouth, aggressive or disrespectful, making social interactions uncomfortable. This perception may result in a secret or public lack of respect from peers, diminished trust, and strained relationships. Additionally, rudeness can create a negative reputation, causing people to avoid or disengage from the rude person. Overall, rudeness tends to foster a hostile environment and can have lasting consequences on personal and professional connections.

Rude people not only make others feel uncomfortable, but undervalued. Their behavior can create feelings of anger, frustration, or sadness in those on the receiving end of their rudeness. Additionally, consistent encounters with rude people can negatively impact a person's self-esteem and overall mood, thus, contributing to a toxic environment that affects the receiver of the rudeness. Rudeness can stem from various sources, including personal stress, frustration, or emotional challenges that lead individuals to lash out. It may also arise from a lack of self-awareness or understanding of social norms and etiquette. Environmental factors, such as a toxic or negative upbringing can also influence rude behavior. In some cases, people may act rudely to assert dominance or control in social situations. Ultimately, how a person treats others, especially in challenging situations, serves as a strong indicator of their character and values.

"Go up, you baldhead!"

In 2 Kings 2:23-24, Elisha, the prophet of God, was on his way to Bethel when a group of young boys approached him and began mocking him without cause or provocation. They shouted repeatedly, *"Go up, you baldhead!"* By ridiculing Elisha's appearance, they showed a clear lack of respect and courtesy toward the man of God. Their words were rude, unkind and uncalled for, a blatant attack on the prophet. I am sure that this rudeness caused Elisha to feel disrespected and insulted. The disregard and lack of respect shown to Elisha ultimately led to severe

> *"When we treat others with kindness, we not only uplift their spirits but also create opportunities for deeper connections."*

consequences for those children. Elisha called down a curse upon them, and two bears came from the woods out of nowhere and mauled forty-two of those boys. This outcome served as a powerful reminder that showing respect is important, especially toward men and women of God. Such rudeness takes minimal effort but leaves lasting negative impressions. In contrast, choosing to be courteous uplifts others and maintains peace, requiring only a little thoughtfulness to show respect. The story emphasized the value of treating others with dignity, and the consequences that can sometimes come when we fail to practice the Law of Honor.

Ultimately, practicing courtesy enriches our lives and the lives of those around us. It creates a ripple effect of positivity and support that can lead to remarkable benefits. Embracing this principle not only nurtures our character but also cultivates a community where kindness is valued, leading to a more compassionate and harmonious existence for everyone involved.

Lessons to Live By:

- One's positive demeanor promotes a receptive and welcoming atmosphere, thus, making interactions more pleasant.

- When someone responds to rudeness with politeness and respect, it can disarm the rude behavior and potentially lead to a shift in the other person's attitude.

- When we treat everyone with kindness, we not only uplift their spirits but also create opportunities for deeper connections.

- Rudeness reflects a lack of consideration for social norms and can damage relationships, creating a negative atmosphere in personal and professional settings.

- Rudeness can stem from various sources, including personal stress, frustration, or emotional challenges that lead individuals to lash out.

- Rudeness may also arise from a lack of self-awareness or understanding of social norms and etiquette.

About Mia Merritt

Dr. Mia Y. Merritt is an accomplished educator, consultant, and prolific writer with over 30 years of experience in the fields of education and leadership. Her diverse background encompasses roles in teaching, administration, and curriculum development, having served as a public-school administrator, Assistant Academic Dean, educational consultant, and college professor. Dr. Merritt has authored over 20 books that span topics such as education, personal development, spirituality, and universal laws, including specialized texts utilized in school districts for ESOL students and those preparing to graduate from high school.

In addition to her academic pursuits, Dr. Merritt is a dynamic speaker and facilitator of professional development seminars, where she inspires educators to foster transformative learning environments. Her commitment to education is complemented by a strong media presence; she has hosted a radio program on WZAB (880 The Biz), contributed insightful articles to the Miami Herald and Sun Sentinel, and currently serves as a crime commentator on the TV show Fatal Attraction. Deeply invested in community service, Dr. Merritt actively engages with various boards and organizations that promote health, wealth, and social justice, advocating for equitable opportunities for all individuals.

Dr. Merritt holds a Doctorate in Organizational Leadership, two Master's Degrees, and a Bachelor's Degree in Education. Her educational philosophy centers on the belief that every learner possesses unique potential and that fostering an inclusive, engaging, and challenging learning environment is essential for empowering students to achieve their fullest capabilities.

Other Books by Dr. Mia Merritt

Destined for Great Things

Destined for Great Things Workbook

Divine Principles/Natural Laws of the Universe

Life After High School

Moments of Reflection (a Daily Journal)

Prosperity is Your Birthright

Releasing Emotional Baggage

The Cost of the Anointing

The Cost of the Anointing Workbook

The Power of Money

The Road to Inner Joy

Traveling the Road to Success

Success Principles